Impressionism: American Gardens on Canvas

Exhibition organized by
The New York Botanical Garden
May 14 – September 11, 2016

Traveling to the Taubman Museum of Art,
Roanoke, Virginia
February 17 – May 14, 2017

NYBG/125

© 2016 The New York Botanical Garden

The New York Botanical Garden
2900 Southern Blvd.
Bronx, NY 10458
nybg.org

All rights reserved. No part of this publication may be reproduced or transmitted in any form or by any means, electronic or mechanical, including photocopy, recording, or any other information storage and retrieval system, or otherwise without written permission from the publisher.

The New York Botanical Garden

Gregory Long
Chief Executive Officer
The William C. Steere Sr. President

This catalog has been published on the occasion of the exhibition *Impressionism: American Gardens on Canvas*, organized by The New York Botanical Garden, May 14–September 11, 2016.
Traveling to the Taubman Museum of Art, Roanoke, Virginia, February 17–May 14, 2017.

Guest Curator and Volume Editor:
Linda S. Ferber

All works and photographs are reproduced courtesy of the creators and lenders of the material depicted. The following images are those for which separate or additional credits are due.

Image credits:
Pages 2–3: William Chadwick, *Irises* (detail), see fig. 40
Fig. 2: Photograph: Princeton University Art Museum/Art Resource, NY
Fig. 3: The New York Botanical Garden
Fig. 4: Photograph © Terra Foundation for American Art, Chicago
Fig. 6: Photograph: Hami Bahadori
Fig. 7: Photograph by Beowulf Sheehan
Fig. 8: Photograph by Travis Fullerton, © Virginia Museum of Fine Arts
Fig. 9: Photograph © Terra Foundation for American Art, Chicago
Fig. 10: Photography by Lee Stalsworth
Fig. 11: Photograph: Princeton University Art Museum/Art Resource, NY
Fig. 16: Photograph © The Metropolitan Museum of Art. Image source: Art Resource, NY
Fig. 17: Photograph © The New-York Historical Society
Fig. 19: Photograph: Katherine Wetzel © Virginia Museum of Fine Arts
Fig. 20: Photograph © Terra Foundation for American Art, Chicago

Fig. 27: Photograph © The Metropolitan Museum of Art. Image source: Art Resource, NY
Fig. 34: Photograph courtesy of Select Fine Art Gallery, Palm Beach FL. selectfine.org
Fig. 42: Image courtesy Acanthus Press
Fig. 47: Photograph © The Metropolitan Museum of Art. Image source: Art Resource, NY
Fig. 50: Photograph ca. 1980–1997, © Massimo Listri/Corbis
Fig. 51: Photograph © Ben Asen Photography
Fig. 52: Photograph © A.J. Kollar Fine Painting, LLC
Pages 78–79: Maria Oakey Dewing, *Rose Garden* (detail), see fig. 10

Printed in U.S.A.

ISBN: 978-0-692-70537-7

Foreword Gregory Long	7
Acknowledgments	9
An American Impressionist Garden Todd A. Forrest	11
American Gardens: A Homegrown Impressionist Subject Linda S. Ferber	17
Sense of Place, Sense of Spirit: Childe Hassam and Celia Thaxter on the Isles of Shoals David Park Curry	39
In Miss Florence's Garden: Edmund Greacen at Old Lyme Susan G. Larkin	51
John Singer Sargent at Vizcaya and Pocantico Hills Elaine Kilmurray	63
Checklist	74
Further Reading	77

FIGURE 1

John H. Twachtman
Wildflowers, ca. 1890
Oil on canvas, 30¼ x 25¼ in.
Taubman Museum of Art
Acquired with funds provided by the
Horace G. Fralin Charitable Trust
and Partial Support from Spanierman
Gallery, LLC (1999.004)

Foreword

Impressionism emerged as an artistic style in the United States in the late 19th century. The artists of this movement, inspired by the work of their European counterparts, employed the brilliant palette and broken strokes that were the hallmarks of Impressionism from its earliest days. Like their European colleagues, they depicted scenes of "modern life," including town and country leisure pursuits. The careers of American Impressionists such as Childe Hassam, William Merritt Chase, John H. Twachtman, and John Singer Sargent coincided with the burgeoning of garden culture in America. In fact, The New York Botanical Garden is one of many cultural institutions founded during this period. Now in its 125th year, its mission is grounded in the same reverence for nature and belief in the power of gardens to improve lives that is expressed in the paintings of the day.

From May 14 to September 11, 2016, The New York Botanical Garden is presenting *Impressionism: American Gardens on Canvas*, which explores the importance of American gardens, from intimate, private spaces at artists' homes to formal estate gardens to public parks, in the work of American Impressionists. Some of these gardens still exist today and are recognized as important cultural sites.

The exhibition in the Enid A. Haupt Conservatory features a typical garden of the turn of the 20th century, reminiscent of the lushly planted Colonial Revival gardens of private residences and art colonies on Long Island and in New England. The gardens of this era were replete with hollyhocks, irises, lilies, peonies, poppies, and many other classic garden plants. Paintings and sculptures by iconic artists, including Hassam, Chase, Sargent, and others, are on display in the LuEsther T. Mertz Library's Art Gallery. A rich suite of programming complements the Conservatory and Library exhibitions, with a poetry walk and poetry readings, film screenings, and live performances of American music. In the Everett Children's Adventure Garden, young visitors can explore the art—and science—of color theory and produce their own Impressionist masterpieces.

For their important contributions to the preparation of this exhibition, I wish to thank: Linda S. Ferber, Ph.D., Guest Curator and Volume Editor, who guided the development of the exhibition from the very beginning; Alice Quinn, Executive Director of the Poetry Society of America, the Garden's longtime partner in themed poetry walks and readings in conjunction with special exhibitions; the institutional lenders of the paintings and sculptures, Crystal Bridges Museum of American Art; Florence Griswold Museum; The Heckscher Museum of Art; Henry Art Gallery, University of Washington, Seattle; Kykuit, The National Trust for Historic Preservation; Memorial Art Gallery of the University of Rochester, N.Y.; The Metropolitan Museum of Art; The New-York Historical Society; Parrish Art Museum; Princeton University Art Museum; Taubman Museum of Art; Terra Foundation for American Art; Virginia Museum of Fine Arts; numerous private collectors; and the public and private funders without whose support *Impressionism: American Gardens on Canvas* would not have been possible.

This exhibition would also not be possible without the generosity of our major funders, including the National Endowment for the Humanities, the National Endowment for the Arts, the LuEsther T. Mertz Charitable Trust, Gillian and Robert Steel, the New York State Council on the Arts, and Bloomberg Philanthropies.

The New York Botanical Garden is uniquely positioned to organize an exhibition exploring the close ties between Impressionism and the gardens of the era. I hope you will be transfixed by the exquisite beauty of the garden settings that inspired these stunning works of art, and that you will immerse yourself in the art of the era that gave birth to some of America's greatest gardens.

Gregory Long
Chief Executive Officer
The William C. Steere Sr. President
The New York Botanical Garden

Acknowledgments

The New York Botanical Garden wishes to thank the following individuals and institutions for their assistance in the development of *Impressionism: American Gardens on Canvas*.

Linda S. Ferber, Ph.D.
Guest Curator and Volume Editor

Poetry Society of America
Alice Quinn, *Executive Director*

Taubman Museum of Art
Della Watkins, *Executive Director*

Warren Adelson
Cynthia Bronson Altman
Frederick Baker
Joel H. Berson
Katherine Bourguignon
Terry A. Carbone
Margi Conrads
Debra Force
Barbara Dayer Gallati
Robert Gunn
Susan A. Hobbs
Margaret Hofer
James M. Keny
Leftwich D. Kimbrough
Elizabeth Kornhauser
Karl Kusserow
Amy Kurtz Lansing
Deirdre Lawrence
Alicia Longwell
Sophie Lynford
Anna O. Marley
Sara Cedar Miller
Amy Moorefield
Elizabeth Oustinoff
Susanne Pandich
Anne dePietro
Paul Provost
Joshua Ruff
Thayer Tolles
Eric Widing
Sylvia Yount

Leadership Support

  LuEsther T. Mertz Charitable Trust   Gillian and Robert Steel   New York State Council on the Arts with the support of Governor Andrew M. Cuomo and the New York State Legislature

Mobile Media supported by Bloomberg Philanthropies

Additional support provided by the Allwin Family Foundation, Milton and Sally Avery Arts Foundation, E.H.A. Foundation, Inc., Anna-Maria and Stephen Kellen Foundation, and New York State Council for the Humanities

Exhibitions in the Enid A. Haupt Conservatory are made possible by the Estate of Enid A. Haupt.

Exhibitions in the Mertz Library are made possible by the LuEsther T. Mertz Charitable Trust.

Additional support for Mertz Library exhibitions has also been provided by The Andrew W. Mellon Foundation and by a Challenge Grant from the National Endowment for the Humanities.

Any views, findings, conclusions, or recommendations expressed in this exhibition do not necessarily represent those of the National Endowment for the Humanities.

Lenders to the Exhibition
Crystal Bridges Museum of American Art
Florence Griswold Museum
The Heckscher Museum of Art
Henry Art Gallery, University of Washington, Seattle
Kykuit, The National Trust for Historic Preservation
Memorial Art Gallery of the University of Rochester
The Metropolitan Museum of Art
Neville-Strass Collection
The New-York Historical Society
Parrish Art Museum
Princeton University Art Museum
Taubman Museum of Art
Terra Foundation for American Art
Douglas Dockery Thomas
Virginia Museum of Fine Arts
Westervelt Collection
Private Collections

Exhibition Advisory Committee
David Park Curry, Ph.D.
Harvey Flad, Ph.D.
William H. Gerdts, Ph.D.
Mac Griswold
May Brawley Hill
Susan G. Larkin, Ph.D.
Marta McDowell
Elizabeth Barlow Rogers
David Schuyler, Ph.D.

An American Impressionist Garden

Todd A. Forrest

What is an American Impressionist garden? It is a garden bursting with old-fashioned flowers—the same cheerful and colorful bulbs, annuals, biennials, and perennials featured in the gardens in vogue at the turn of the 20th century. It is a warm and welcoming garden, meant to be lived in and tinkered with rather than simply observed. It is the bright, lushly planted garden style that inspired American Impressionists. It is what Francisca Coelho and the Horticulture staff at The New York Botanical Garden set out to create in the Enid A. Haupt Conservatory for *Impressionism: American Gardens on Canvas*.

To design our American Impressionist garden, we began with a close examination of the paintings Guest Curator Linda S. Ferber considered for inclusion in the exhibition. Some of the paintings depicted the formal gardens created by Gilded Age Industrialists, such as John Singer Sargent's 1917 watercolors of Vizcaya, James Deering's Italianate garden in Miami, and Kykuit, the Rockefeller estate in Pocantico Hills, New York. Others provided a gardenesque perspective on a natural landscape, including William Merritt Chase's *Landscape: Shinnecock, Long Island*, which depicts the wildflowers and grasses of Long Island dunes [fig. 2].

While we considered formal gardens and wild landscapes as inspiration for our American Impressionist garden, we were ultimately drawn to the most often repeated subject of the assembled works—informal, abundant flower gardens vibrant with color. We saw windblown poppies and hollyhocks in Childe Hassam's depiction of Celia Thaxter's garden on Appledore Island, in Maine, seven miles off the coast of New Hampshire. We saw lush beds of irises in a work by William Chadwick. We saw phlox in paintings that artists made of their own gardens: John H. Twachtman in Connecticut and Hugh Henry Breckenridge in Pennsylvania. We saw that, like the leading gardeners of the era, American Impressionists were seduced by lilies, peonies, rhododendrons, azaleas, roses, goldenrods, and dozens of other flowers.

> "A garden, large or small, must be treated in an impressionist manner."
>
> Beatrix Farrand, 1907

FIGURE 2

William Merritt Chase
Landscape: Shinnecock, Long Island
(detail), see fig. 11

FIGURE 3

Celia Thaxter's poppies were immortalized in the paintings of Childe Hassam and other summer visitors.

Inspired, we set out to learn as much as we could about gardening trends at the turn of the 20th century. This was a time of transition for American horticulture. The bedding-out of tender annuals and tropicals, which had spread from European public parks and grand estates during the Victorian era, was considered overwrought and un-American by the most creative gardeners of the day. Articles in *Country Life in America, Garden and Forest, Scribner's,* and other taste-making periodicals called for a more distinctly American gardening culture, one that celebrated the beauty, fragrance, and picturesque nature of old-fashioned flowers grown in the dooryard gardens of the colonial era [fig. 3].

Old-fashioned flower gardens were the perfect subject for American Impressionist artists, who captured the essence of domestic life with painterly brushstrokes and brilliant color [fig. 4]. Many of the most important artists of the period painted and gardened at artist's colonies in rural and suburban locations such as Cos Cob and Old Lyme, Connecticut and East Hampton, Long Island. Poet Celia Thaxter presided over an impressive group of musicians, writers, and artists who visited her family's resort on Appledore Island. Thaxter's guests particularly enjoyed the exuberant old-fashioned garden she created adjacent to her summer cottage on Appledore. At their behest, in 1894 she published *An Island Garden,* a deeply personal account of a gardening year on Appledore illustrated with chromolithographs of charming watercolors by Childe Hassam.

Alternating between poetic descriptions of her beloved flowers and detailed accounts of her horticultural activities from sowing poppy seeds to releasing toads to control the rapacious slugs that were feasting on her plants, *An Island Garden* provided us with a wealth of information about an American Impressionist garden. Although Thaxter's garden was quite small (750 square feet), she incorporated an impressive diversity of bulbs, annuals, biennials, perennials, and vines into its beds and borders. Thaxter described the plants in her garden as "mostly the old fashioned flowers our grandmothers loved."

The plants in an American Impressionist garden are resilient, cheerful, and free-flowering. In early spring, snowdrops emerge through just-thawed soil, followed by crocuses, daffodils, and squills. Any open ground is filled with pansies, violets, wallflowers, Iceland poppies, and other cool-season annuals. As the weather warms, spires of larkspur, foxglove, phlox, and hollyhocks rise above peonies, lavender, penstemon, and roses. Climbing roses, clematis, sweet pea, and morning glories clamber over trellises and simple wooden fences.

FIGURE 4

Hugh Henry Breckenridge
White Phlox (detail, see fig. 9), 1906
Oil on canvas, 30 x 25 in.
Terra Foundation for American Art
Daniel J. Terra Collection
(1988.15)

> This element of chance must have been appreciated by a group of artists seeking to capture snapshots of daily life on their canvases.

In late summer, dahlias, asters, and sunflowers extend the flowering season. Plants are allowed to self-seed and intermingle, creating unforeseen and welcome combinations. This element of chance must have been appreciated by a group of artists seeking to capture snapshots of daily life on their canvases.

The paintings also taught us that the American Impressionist garden is often intimate and usually associated with a house. Theodore Wores's painting of fellow artist Thomas Moran's old-fashioned garden offers glimpses of the nearby house with its gabled roof and shaded porch [fig. 5]. Matilda Browne's *In Voorhees's Garden* shows a young girl admiring profuse flower borders in a garden planted next to a house with white clapboards and a porch. Hassam's illustrations for *An Island Garden* reveal that Celia Thaxter's garden was an extension of her home. Steps lead from Thaxter's front door directly into her garden and vines planted in the garden create a living green wall along the side of the house. Thaxter cut openings into this tangle of foliage to provide views from her porch of the garden and the landscape beyond. The shared love of writer and artist for this landscape is evident to those who read her book or view his paintings.

We found inspiration for our American Impressionist garden in each of the paintings we studied. Our borders burst with Chadwick's irises, Twachtman's phlox, Browne's peonies, and other perennials our great-great-great-grandmothers loved. Biennial foxgloves, larkspurs, and mulleins provide scale and drama. The constant addition of a suite of tried-and-true annuals ensures exuberant color from earliest spring to first frost. Clematis and climbing roses scramble over rustic four-board fences and climb the facade of a simple country house. Our American Impressionist garden even has a porch with rocking chairs and a view of all the flowers—the perfect prospect for an artist looking to capture brilliant color in fleeting light.

Todd A. Forrest
Arthur Ross Vice President for
Horticulture and Living Collections
The New York Botanical Garden

FIGURE 5

Theodore Wores
*Thomas Moran's House
(East Hampton, Long Island)*, ca. 1894
Oil on canvas board, 9 x 12 in.
The Heckscher Museum of Art
Gift of Dr. A. Jess Shenson in memory
of Ronald G. Pisano

FIGURE 6

Childe Hassam
*Old House and Garden,
East Hampton, Long Island,* 1898
Oil on canvas, 24 1/16 x 20 in.
Henry Art Gallery, University of
Washington, Seattle
Horace C. Henry Collection
(26.70)

American Gardens:
A Homegrown Impressionist Subject

Linda S. Ferber, Ph.D.

Impressionism emerged in France during the 1860s. The established style was distinguished by the use of brilliant colors applied with vigorous brushstrokes to capture the "impression" of a subject painted in the open air. Impressionism was associated with modern life subjects: recording the social rituals and pastimes of a largely urban and bourgeois society. These included views in Parisian gardens and parks, as well as scenes of leisure painted on expeditions into the French countryside.[1] Claude Monet's garden at Giverny has gained worldwide fame today that is nearly equal to that of his painterly interpretations of the site. By the late 1880s, Impressionism had become an international phenomenon embraced by many American artists who painted abroad, some in Giverny and at other sites. Returning to the United States, they adapted Impressionism to subjects that reflected the tastes of American audiences. "What made American Impressionism American," it has been observed, "was not *how* they painted…but *what* they painted: subjects that were specifically, self-consciously, intentionally American."[2] They painted the urban spectacle of rapidly growing cities as well as old farms and colonial villages in the countryside. And among these homegrown subjects was the American garden.

The generally positive reception of Impressionism in the United States coincided with the burgeoning garden culture in the suburban and country retreats of middle- and upper-class Americans. Impressionism's introduction also corresponded with a broad shift in the national ideology about the American's relationship to nature. Cultural preference turned from landscape images celebrating the majestic frontier wilderness as seen in the paintings of the Hudson River School to portrayals of the inhabited landscape and expression of nostalgia for pre-industrial communities and simpler ways of life. The Impressionists' interpretations of well-tended residential gardens and parklands resonated with contemporary American beliefs about the "good life." These ideals of health and moral well-being were embodied in paintings that portrayed domesticated nature as a retreat offering respite from the perceived pressures of rapid social,

"What made American Impressionism American was not how they painted… but what they painted."

demographic, and economic changes that characterized modern life in the United States.³

It is not surprising to find domestic gardens and parks among the most popular American Impressionist subjects. Gardens cultivated purely for aesthetic enjoyment were perceived as creative endeavors in themselves, serving as generative sites for the artist's plein-air (open air) painting and for the gardener's horticultural skills. Some artists were themselves gardeners. "The two arts of painting and garden design are closely related[....]A garden, large or small, must be treated in an impressionist manner," wrote landscape designer Beatrix Farrand in her 1907 article, "The Garden as a Picture." Imagist poet Amy Lowell went further in her "Impressionist Picture of a Garden," envisioning poet, painter, and gardener united under the banner of Impressionism. "Give me sunlight, cupped in a paint brush" she declared, "And smear the red of peonies/Over my garden…."⁴

FIGURE 7

Mary Fairchild MacMonnies Low
View of Dusenberry Gardens,
after 1910
Oil on canvas, 30 x 25 in.
Collection of
Douglas Dockery Thomas

The Colonial Revival: Grandmother's Garden

Lowell's poem conjures an old-fashioned garden modeled on the informal dooryard gardens of the Colonial period, which was perhaps the prevailing style of the era. This preference reflected the continuing influence of Colonial Revival styles generated around the 1876 Philadelphia Centennial Exposition and accelerated by the 1893 World's Columbian Exposition. Revival enthusiasts, both nostalgic and nativist, celebrated Colonial and Federal America as cultural and artistic ideals. They revered images of long-inhabited terrains and vernacular buildings with picturesque architectural features, often set in dooryard gardens.⁵ These were enclosed by fences, hedges, or low walls and densely planted with classic garden plants such as hollyhocks, irises, and peonies. Such brilliant masses of blooms and foliage under strong sunlight presented artists with ample opportunities for plein-air painting.

California Impressionist Theodore Wores (1859–1939) visited Western landscape painter Thomas Moran in East Hampton on Long Island around 1894 when he painted Moran's Queen Anne-style studio house and garden.⁶ The house was barely ten years old, but surrounded by the blooms and vines of Mary Moran's old-fashioned garden, it might have been there for decades [fig. 5].

Many prominent painters, writers, and architects lived and worked in Bronxville, New York, in the picturesque turn-of-the-century enclave of Lawrence Park. Mary Fairchild MacMonnies Low

FIGURE 8

Daniel Putnam Brinley
The Peony Garden, 1912
Oil on canvas, 45 ¾ x 38 ¾ in.
Virginia Museum of
Fine Arts, Richmond
Adolph D. and Wilkins C.
Williams Fund

FIGURE 9

Hugh Henry Breckenridge
White Phlox, 1906
Oil on canvas, 30 x 25 in.
Terra Foundation for American Art
Daniel J. Terra Collection (1988.15)

joined her new husband, fellow artist Will Low, there in 1910 after a decade and a half of residence in Giverny. There her renowned garden at a converted priory had provided the environment for many paintings [fig. 33]. As in France, she painted and gardened in Bronxville. Not surprisingly, she was drawn to the gardens at the historic Masterson-Dusenberry House where she deftly chronicled the hollyhocks, dahlias and cosmos flourishing in a sunlit corner of the garden [fig. 7].[7]

Around 1903 Impressionist Clark G. Voorhees purchased a colonial house in the historic Connecticut town of Old Lyme where his wife, Maude Folsom, created traditional gardens. In 1914 Voorhees's fellow Impressionist Matilda Browne painted the house, called Ker Guen, nestled in its summer garden [fig. 41].[8] Daniel Putnam Brinley rented a property called Blanchards in the Connecticut retreat area known as Silvermine. The old house rises behind a sprawling bed of peonies filling more than half the canvas with broadly brushed blossoms [fig. 8]. Brinley's radical perspective and dense semi-abstract patterning of brushstrokes were advanced techniques and remind us that Impressionism was identified as a modern movement.[9] *The Peony Garden* was shown in the New York Armory Show of 1913 where avant-garde European and American artists exhibited together. His fellow Impressionists Childe Hassam, Ernest Lawson, and John H. Twachtman also participated.[10]

> Many of the American Impressionists featured in this exhibition were active gardeners.

Outdoor Studios: The Artist's Garden

Many of the American Impressionists featured in this exhibition were active gardeners. Their gardens reflected the range of garden design styles and plants popular in the period.

The gardens of Clark Voorhees (portrayed by his fellow artist Browne) and Hugh Henry Breckenridge were domestic and informal, deriving their beauty from densely planted flower beds bursting with color. Breckenridge's suburban residence in historic Fort Washington, Pennsylvania was the site of a plein-air summer school. The artist built Phloxdale, a studio house celebrating the exuberant old-fashioned blooms that dominated his gardens [fig. 9]. There, he painted floral subjects to great critical praise and taught plein-air painting classes.[11] In contrast, muralist William de Leftwich Dodge's grounds at Villa Francesca, his Long Island estate, were formal and architectural, evoking European estate gardens [fig. 14]. In every instance these gardens provided opportunities for the plein-air painting that was central to Impressionism.

John H. Twachtman created a unique woodland and streamside garden at his farm in Greenwich, Connecticut. In 1889 Twachtman settled there, commuting to teach in New York City. The artist dedicated himself for more than a decade to refining Willow Brook into a private realm that included a winding steam and gardens around the farmhouse, sites recorded in many paintings.[12] In *Wildflowers* [fig. 1] Twachtman focuses closely on his chosen subject, immersing the viewer in the natural world of floral life captured here in the artist's dense tapestry of delicately colored brushstrokes. Maria Oakey Dewing and her artist-husband, Thomas Wilmer Dewing, were avid gardeners and horticulturists during their 1885 to 1903 summer residence in Cornish, New Hampshire. Dewing was famous in her day as an innovative painter of closely observed flowers *in situ*, a vision realized after what she described as a "long apprenticeship in the garden." In *Rose Garden* she presses the viewer to share her experience of the horticultural world from the kneeling gardener's point of view [fig. 10].[13]

Summer Retreats: Gardens at Art Colonies

The Dewings were central figures in the Cornish art colony. At their summer residence, Doveridge, they cultivated indigenous plants and Maria "painted constantly in my garden."[14] The couple were among many artists who left cities in the summer to work at picturesque sites across the Northeast. The natural landscapes and residential gardens around these suburbs and villages provided ample subjects for plein-air painting.[15] Some, such as William Merritt Chase and Breckenridge, conducted outdoor painting schools, drawing populations of students. Camaraderie prevailed as well as a lively intellectual milieu. Among the best-known summer art colonies were Appledore, Maine; the East End of Long Island, New York; and Old Lyme, Connecticut.

From 1890 to 1894, and for many summers thereafter, Childe Hassam was a regular summer visitor to Appledore Island in the Isles of Shoals, an archipelago that extends along both sides of the border between Maine and New Hampshire. As David Park Curry writes in his essay in this volume, Hassam joined a summer community that revolved around Celia Thaxter, who was both a poet and a dedicated gardener. There, Hassam explored opportunities for plein-air painting under brilliant coastal light, inspired by the riot of colors in Thaxter's old-fashioned seaside garden.[16]

Picturesque colonial architecture set in the light-filled Long Island landscape made for another ideal summer destination. In 1891 William Merritt Chase began to summer at Shinnecock Hills, an

FIGURE 10

Maria Oakey Dewing
Rose Garden, 1901
Oil on canvas, 24 x 40 ½ in.
Crystal Bridges Museum of
American Art, Bentonville, Arkansas
(2006.67)

Impressionism: American Gardens on Canvas

FIGURE 11

William Merritt Chase
Landscape: Shinnecock,
Long Island ca. 1896
Oil on wood panel, 14 5/16 x 16 1/8 in.
Princeton University Art Museum
Gift of Francis A. Comstock,
Class of 1919 (y1939–35)

expanse of barren dunes on the Atlantic coast populated by windswept trees and shrubs. He conducted an outdoor art school there from 1891 to 1902 and painted innovative landscapes. These brilliant paintings often included views of the artist's shingle-style studio house designed for him by architect Stanford White, and featured family members in white dresses and fanciful bonnets who performed as the floral elements in Chase's wild and lyrical seaside landscapes [fig. 11].[17] In 1898 Childe Hassam first visited East Hampton, where he was inspired to paint a series of colonial houses in the village [fig. 6]. Hassam's web of brilliantly hued brushstrokes conjured the weatherworn facade of a shingled house embowered behind sheltering trees and the abundant plantings of a colonial dooryard garden.

Hassam had admired Old Lyme on his first visit as "a pretty fine old town."[18] Boarding with Florence Griswold, the artist was a powerful though intermittent presence between 1903 to 1909 at this popular summer painting colony on the Connecticut coast. Miss Florence's grand ancestral home was the center of artistic activity with a cordial hostess as well as extensive grounds and gardens for painting out of doors. As Susan Larkin tells us in her essay, Hassam's arrival sparked the recognition of this colonial village as an Impressionist commune. His presence might have drawn Edmund William Greacen who painted a series of works portraying views in Griswold's famous gardens [fig. 32]. William Chadwick first visited Old Lyme in the summer of 1902, settling there in 1915. His experiments with landscape painting and Impressionism included the lush irises in his own garden [fig. 40].[19] Griswold encouraged the artists who lived in Old Lyme to garden.[20] In this spirit, Matilda Browne portrayed a bank of red and white peonies winding across a sunlit lawn [fig. 12]. A young woman in summer white bends above the bed, her hat echoing the blossoms and evoking the long tradition linking women with the garden's fecundity and beauty.[21]

Impressionists in the Formal Garden

In contrast to the old-fashioned gardens gracing suburban residences and country houses were the large formal gardens of the era. Wealthy patrons worked closely with landscape architects and nurserymen to create American versions of the grand European estates. In addition to decorous plantings, formal gardens included architectural elements such as pergolas, balustrades, fountains, and garden sculpture. These

> Picturesque colonial architecture set in the light-filled Long Island landscape made for another ideal summer destination.

FIGURE 12

Matilda Browne
Peonies, 1907
Oil on panel, 11 ½ x 14 in.
Florence Griswold Museum
Purchase (2013.11)

FIGURE 13

Ernest Lawson
The Garden, 1914
Oil on canvas, 20 x 24 in.
Memorial Art Gallery of the
University of Rochester
Gift of the Estate of Emily and
James Sibley Watson (51.36)

Impressionism: American Gardens on Canvas

FIGURE 14

William de Leftwich Dodge
The Artist's Garden, ca. 1916
Oil on canvas, 35 x 27 in.
Neville-Strass Collection

private precincts were not readily accessible, so the paintings under discussion here were generally associated with artist commissions from moneyed patrons. Although an expatriate, John Singer Sargent painted portraits of many American sitters abroad and in the United States. In 1917 the artist painted John D. Rockefeller and visited Charles and James Deering, brothers with estates in Florida. While in residence, as Elaine Kilmurray writes in her essay, Sargent also painted out of doors in their formal gardens, a habit that had persisted long after his first engagement with French Impressionism in the 1880s [figs. 45, 47, 48, 50, 51].

Ernest Lawson was likely commissioned to paint a terrace garden belonging to Mr. and Mrs. Horace Huddleston Rogers, Jr. in the exclusive residential preserve at Tuxedo Park, New York [fig 13]. The restrained luxury of these private grounds was conceived by architects Walker & Gillette in the Italianate manner as an alfresco "garden room." A massive stucco retaining wall defined the terrace and at its terminus formed a colonnaded tea house and a grotto. Beside the wall, a reflecting pool lined with blue tiles mirrored the surrounding foliage and plantings. While the subject is an unusual one for the artist, Lawson's portrayal manifests his distinctive Impressionist style, a painterly technique described as a "palette of crushed jewels."[22]

In 1906 renowned muralist William de Leftwich Dodge built a studio house overlooking Setauket Bay in a fanciful classical style. A visitor described Villa Francesca as "a bit of ancient Greece set down on the shore of Long Island Sound." The artist's terraced formal gardens and intricate pergolas inspired a series of Impressionist landscapes. *The Artist's Garden* reflected Dodge's social ambitions; a glimpse of the terrace balustrade hints at the grandeur of the house [fig. 14]. His easel is set low, immersing the viewer in rose gardens and networks of trellises and pergolas under dappled sunlight. A classical bearded piping Pan figure commands the fountain pool signaling the importance of sculpture as a highlight of the formal garden.[23]

The plant-filled atrium at Villa Francesca housed a marble torso then thought to be antique and a mosaic fountain featuring Frederick W. MacMonnies's boyish *Pan of Rohallion*, a gift from MacMonnies to Dodge [fig. 15]. MacMonnies had originated his large Pan figure at Stanford White's request in 1889 for the country estate garden of Rohallion, built by financier Edward Dean Adams in Sea Bright (now Rumson), New Jersey.[24] Henri Crenier's animated *Boy and Turtle* [fig. 16] was created as a fountain figure whose

FIGURE 15

Frederick W. MacMonnies
Pan of Rohallion, 1890
Bronze, 29 3/4 x 9 x 10 1/2 in.
Memorial Art Gallery of the University of Rochester, Anonymous gift (98.68)

Impressionism: American Gardens on Canvas

FIGURE 16

Henri Crenier
Boy and Turtle, 1912
Bronze, 19 ¾ x 11 x 11 in.
The Metropolitan Museum of Art
Amelia B. Lazarus Fund, 1913
(13.87)

life-size version presides in Baltimore's Mount Vernon Place, a park designed by Carrère and Hastings to flank Robert Mills's Washington Monument.[24] Both MacMonnies and Crenier were trained in France, excelling in such highly naturalistic bronze figures. These dynamic youths, like Anna Hyatt Huntington's elegant *Diana of the Chase*, were conceived as evocative features for formal gardens where encounters with classical and mythological figures inspired memories of European gardens and parks [fig. 17].[26]

Impressionists in the Park: Public Gardens in America

In addition to painting the private gardens created by the growing leisure class in the late 19th century, American Impressionists also painted the progressive public parks that were planned in response to the rapid growth and industrialization of American cities. Public parks were instruments of civic pride intended to provide the urban masses with the same healthful and morally refining encounters with nature that private gardens offered for people of means. Parks were also highly charged social spaces where urban populations of all classes, ages, and genders interacted at leisure in open air settings that were ideal for artists such as Chase and Hassam who were interested in both outdoor painting and modern life.[27] Both artists were masters of Impressionist visual strategies employed to interpret these American public gardens, artfully exploiting perspectives of walkways and shadow patterns across sunlit lawns to create dynamic paintings.

William Merritt Chase was first among American Impressionists to focus on the American park as a signature subject. When newly married, he and his wife resided for a time in Brooklyn where Chase created a series of brilliant paintings portraying nearby Tompkins Park [fig. 18]. The rectangular site, no more than three blocks long, was designed by Frederick Law Olmsted and Calvert Vaux (also the designers of Brooklyn's much larger Prospect Park) in a formal manner with perimeter plantings, gravel walks, and a central lawn with trees. The small park was a retreat for neighborhood residents whose row houses are visible just beyond the edge of the park.

Hassam's home was New York City, and his urban views included depictions of Central Park. The most famous of American parks, Central Park had been innovatively designed by Olmsted and Vaux to accommodate cross-town traffic in a concealed fashion that gave pedestrians the impression of entering a rural enclave. Hassam's image of women and children descending a gracefully curving stairway

FIGURE 17

Anna Vaughn Hyatt Huntington
Diana of the Chase, 1922
Bronze and marble, 99 x 33 x 29 ½ in.
The New-York Historical Society
Gift of Mr. and Mrs. Archer B.
Huntington (1939.252)

FIGURE 18

William Merritt Chase
Park in Brooklyn, ca. 1887
Oil on panel, 16 1/8 x 24 1/8 in.
Parrish Art Museum, Water Mill,
New York, Littlejohn Collection
(1961.5.11)

reinforces the vision of a wooded pastoral retreat, as does a pair of swans gliding on the placid body of water [fig. 19].[28]

Hassam's *Horticulture Building, World's Columbian Exposition, Chicago* [fig. 20] was intended for a souvenir publication celebrating the Beaux Arts grandeur of Chicago's White City, the setting for the 1893 World's Columbian Exposition. While Hassam visited Chicago in 1892, his images of the fair, which did not open until 1893, were based on architect's drawings. From these, the artist created a convincing rendering of well-dressed fairgoers on a sunny day enjoying respite on The Wooded Island, Olmsted's park in The Lagoon.[29] Beyond them, the colossal central conservatory dome of the Horticulture Building rises in the distance like a radiant vision, long gone, yet echoed today in the magnificent Enid A. Haupt Conservatory at The New York Botanical Garden.

FIGURE 19

Childe Hassam
Descending the Steps, Central Park, 1895
Oil on canvas, 22 3/8 x 22 1/4 in.
Virginia Museum of Fine Arts, Richmond
Gift of the Estate of
Hildegarde Graham van Roijen
(93.112)

FIGURE 20

Childe Hassam
Horticulture Building, World's Columbian Exposition, Chicago, 1893
Oil on canvas, 18 1/2 x 26 1/4 in.
Terra Foundation for American Art
Daniel J. Terra Collection (1999.67)

LINDA S. FERBER, Ph.D.,
Guest Curator and Volume Editor
for *Impressionism: American Gardens on Canvas*, is Senior Art Historian and Museum Director Emerita,
The New-York Historical Society.

1. For more on French Impressionism, see: Robert L. Herbert, *Impressionism: Art, Leisure, and Parisian Society* (New Haven CT: Yale University Press, 1988); Richard Brettell, Scott Schaefer et al, *A Day in the Country: Impressionism and the French Landscape* (Los Angeles CA: Los Angeles County Museum of Art, 1984); T. J. Clark, *The Painting of Modern Life: Paris in the Art of Manet and his Followers* (Princeton NJ: Princeton University Press, 1984).

2. H. Barbara Weinberg, Doreen Bolger, and David Park Curry, *American Impressionism and Realism: The Painting of Modern Life, 1885–1915* (New York: The Metropolitan Museum of Art, 1994), 25.

3. This shift in cultural preference is discussed in Lisa N. Peters, "Cultivated Wilderness and Remote Accessibility: American Impressionist Views of the Home and its Grounds," and David Schuyler, "Old Dwellings, Traditional Landscapes: Impressionist Artists and the Rediscovery of American Places," in Lisa N. Peters and Peter M. Lukehart, eds., *Visions of Home: American Impressionist Images of Suburban Leisure and Country Comfort* (Carlisle, PA: The Trout Gallery, Dickinson College distributed by the University Press of New England, 1997), 9–33, 34–52 (hereafter cited as Peters and Lukehart, 1997); Kathleen Pyne, "Social Conflict and American Painting in the Age of Darwin," in Donald Keyes and Janice Simone, eds., *Crosscurrents in American Impressionism at the Turn of the Century* (Athens: Georgia Museum of Art, University of Georgia, 1993), 73–99; William H. Gerdts, *American Impressionism* (New York: Abbeville Publishing, 1984),11–15.

4. Beatrix Jones [Farrand], "The Garden as a Picture," *Scribner's Magazine* 42, no. 1 (July 1907), 2, 6; Amy Lowell, "Impressionist Picture of a Garden," from *Pictures of the Floating World* (Boston: Houghton Mifflin, 1919), 128. For the American artist colony in Giverny, see William H. Gerdts, *Monet's Giverny: An Impressionist Colony* (New York: Abbeville, 1993).

5. For the old-fashioned garden and national identity, see Virginia Grace Tuttle, " 'A Desperately Aesthetic Business': Garden Art in America," in Anna O. Marley, *The Artist's Garden: American Impressionism and the Garden Movement* (Philadelphia: University of Pennsylvania Press in association with the Pennsylvania Academy of the Fine Arts, 2015), 27–42; May Brawley Hill, 'For the Scent of Present Fragrance and the Perfume of Olden Times,': The Domestic Garden in American Impressionist Painting," in Peters and Lukehart,1997, 53–68; May Brawley Hill, *Grandmother's Garden: The Old-Fashioned American Garden, 1865–1915* (New York: Harry N. Abrams, Inc., 1995).

6. Robert Hefner and Rosanne Barons, "The Studio: The Home and Workshop of Thomas Moran and Mary Nimmo Moran, 229 Maine Street, East Hampton, N.Y., Historic Structure Report" (East Hampton, 2009), 8, 117. Thanks to Peter Wolfe for making this unpublished document available; Ronald G. Pisano, *Long Island Landscape Painting: 1820–1920* (Boston: New York Graphic Society in association with Little, Brown and Company, 1985), 96–98, 102; Hill, *Grandmother's Garden*, 1995, 48, 49; Lisa N. Peters, "Theodore Wores," in Peters and Lukehart, 1997, 108–109.

7. Mary and Frederick MacMonnies divorced in 1909. She was known thereafter as Mary Fairchild Low. The single-family "cottages" in Lawrence Park were designed in the 1890s by W. W. Kent and William A. Bates. Today Lawrence Park is listed on the National Register of Historic Places, as is the Greek-Revival Masterson-Dusenberry House in Bronxville. For Mary Fairchild MacMonnies Low see: May Brawley Hill, *The American Impressionists in the Garden*, 2, 5–7, 36–39; Kirstin Ringelberg, *Redefining Gender in American Impressionist Studio Paintings* (Burlington, VT: Ashgate, 2010), passim; Kathleen Adler, Erica E. Hirschler, and H. Barbara Weinberg, *Americans in Paris, 1860–1900* (London: National Gallery, 2006); May Brawley Hill, *On Foreign Soil: American Gardeners Abroad* (New York: Harry N. Abrams, Publishers, 2005), pp. 62 -65; Joyce Henri Robinson, Derrick R. Cartwright, E. Adina Gordon, *An Interlude in Giverny* (University Park, PA, Palmer Museum of Art & Giverny, France: Terra Foundation for the Arts, 2000), passim; William H. Gerdts, *Monet's Giverny: An Impressionist Colony*, 132–137, 218, 246; Loretta Hoagland et al, *Lawrence Park: Bronxville's Turn-of-the-Century Art Colony* (Bronxville, NY: Lawrence Park Hilltop Association, 1992), pp. 40–43, 184–186; Barbara Ball Buff, *The Artists of Bronxville, 1890–1930* (Yonkers: Hudson River Museum, 1989); Robert Preato et al, *The Genius of the Fair Muse: Painting and Sculpture Celebrating American Women Artists 1875 to 1945* (New York: Grand Central Galleries, 1987), pp. 38, 66; Mary Smart, "Sunshine and Shade: Mary Fairchild MacMonnies Low," *Woman's Art Journal* 4 (Fall 1983–Winter 1984): 22–25.

8. Browne painted an earlier view of Voorhees's house around 1905. (see: Jeffrey Andersen, William H. Gerdts, and Helen A. Harrison, *En Plein Air: The Art Colonies at East Hampton and Old Lyme, 1880-1930* (East Hampton, NY and Old Lyme, CT: Guild Hall of East Hampton, Inc. / Lyme Historical Society, Inc., 1989), 39–40; Lisa N. Peters, "Clark Greenwood Voorhees," in Peters and Lukehart, 100–101; David Schuyler in Peters and Lukehart, 1997, 46,47; May Brawley Hill, *The American Impressionists in the Garden* (Nashville TN: Cheekwood Botanical Garden & Museum of Art in association with Vanderbilt University Press, 2010). For Browne, see note 23.

9. Lisa N. Peters, "Daniel Putnam Brinley" in Peters and Lukehart, 122–123; May Brawley Hill in Peters and Lukehart,1997, 64; Harold Spencer, Susan G. Larkin, Jeffrey W. Andersen, *Connecticut and American Impressionism* (Storrs, CT: William Benton Museum of Art, 1980), 153–154.

10. For the complete Armory Show checklist, see Marilyn Satin Kushner and Kimberly Orcutt, eds. *The Armory Show at 100: Modernism and Revolution* (New York: New-York Historical Society Museum & Library in association with D Giles Limited, London, 2013): 434–463.

11. Anna O. Marley, "Producing Pictures without Brushes: American Artists and Their Gardens," in Marley, *The Artist's Garden*, 13, 20–21; Lisa N. Peters, "Hugh Henry Breckenridge," in Peters and Lukehart, 138; May Brawley Hill, *The American Impressionists in the Garden*, 21; Lewis and Trudy Keen, *A Brief History of Fort Washington: From Farmland to Suburb* (Charleston, SC: The History Press, 2006), 36–38.

12. Anna O. Marley, "Producing Pictures without Brushes: American Artists and Their Gardens," in Marley, *The Artist's Garden*, 14–15; Susan G. Larkin, *The Cos Cob Colony: Impressionists on the Connecticut Shore* (New Haven: Yale University Press, 2001), passim; Lisa N. Peters, *John Henry Twachtman: An American Impressionist* (Atlanta: High Museum of Art distributed by Hudson Hills Press, New York, 1999): 93–111; Lisa Peters, "Twachtman's Greenwich Paintings: Context and Chronology," in Deborah Chotner, Lisa Peters, Kathleen Pyne, *John Twachtman: Connecticut Landscapes* (National Gallery of Art, Washington DC, 1989) 13–47; Lisa N. Peters, "Twachtman's Greenwich Garden," in Lisa N. Peters, William H. Gerdts, and others, *In the Sunlight: The Floral and Figurative Art of J. H. Twachtman* (New York: Spanierman Gallery, 1989), 11–20.

13. In her 1915 article, "Flower Painters and What the Flower offers to Art," Dewing wrote, "If one would realize the powerful appeal that flowers make to art let them bind themselves to a long apprenticeship in a garden." (*Art and Progress*, VI, no. 8 (June 1915), 262). For Dewing, see Anna O. Marley "Producing Pictures without Brushes: American Artists and their Gardens," and Erin Leary, " 'A Tendency to Outstrip Native Blossoms in Life's Race': Nativism in Impressionist Gardens," in Marley, *The Artist's Garden*, 16–17, 68–70; Linda Merrill, "Maria Oakey Dewing (1845–1927): *Rose Garden*, 1901," in *Celebrating The American Spirit: Masterworks from Crystal Bridges Museum of American Art* (New York: Hudson Hills Press in association with Crystal Bridges Museum of American Art, 2011), 162–163; Susan A. Hobbs, "Maria Oakey Dewing's Flowers and Figures," *The Magazine Antiques*, CLXV, no. 1 (January 2004), 152–159; Ella M. Foshay, *Reflections of Nature: Flowers in American Art* (New York: Alfred A. Knopf, Inc, 1984), 59–62; William H. Gerdts, *Down Garden Paths: The Floral Environment in American Art* (Teaneck: Fairleigh Dickinson Press, 1983), 72–75; Jennifer A Martin, "The Rediscovery of Maria Oakey Dewing," *The Feminist Art Journal* (Summer 1976), 24–27.

14. Cited in Hobbs, op cit, 156, 159, n.20. For the artists' colony at Cornish, see John H. Dryfhout, "The Cornish Colony," and Frances Grimes, "Reminiscences" in *A Circle of Friends: Art Colonies of Cornish and Dublin* (Durham, NH: The University Art Galleries, University of New Hampshire, 1985), 33–58, 59–72.

15. For American Impressionist summer colonies, see: Susan G. Larkin, *The Cos Cob Art Colony* ; Deborah Epstein Solon and Will South, *Colonies of American Impressionism: Cos Cob, Old Lyme, Shinnecock and Laguna Beach* (Laguna Beach CA: Laguna Art Museum); 1999; Thomas Andrew Denenberg and Tracie Felker, "The Art Colonies of Old New England," CLX, no. 4, *The Magazine Antiques* (April 1999), 558–565; Andersen, Gerdts, and Harrison, *The Art Colonies at East Hampton and Old Lyme, 1880–1930*; Spencer, Larkin and Andersen, *Connecticut and American Impressionism*, 1980.

16. David Park Curry, *Childe Hassam: An Island Garden Revisited* (New York: W. W. Norton & Company, 1990); Alan C. Braddock, "Home of the Hummingbird: Thaxter, Hassam, and the Aesthetics of Nature Painted, Planted, and Printed: Chromolithography and Impressionism in America," in Marley, The *Artist's Garden*, 85–87; Susan G. Larkin, "Hassam in New England: Appledore," in Weinberg et al, *Childe Hassam*, 120–145; Gerdts, " A World of Flowers," in Warren Adelson, Jay E. Cantor, William H. Gerdts, *Childe Hassam: Impressionist* (New York: Abbeville Press Publishers, 1999), 178–193 passim; Gerdts, *American Impressionism* (1984): 99–104.

17. Barbara Dayer Gallati, *William Merritt Chase: Modern American Landscapes, 1886–1890* (New York: Brooklyn Museum of Art in association with Harry N. Abrams, Inc. Publishers, 2000); 71–78; Lisa N. Peters, "William Merritt Chase," in Peters and Lukehart, eds., *Visions of Home*, 116, 118; D. Scott Atkinson and Nicolai Cikovsky, Jr., *William Merritt Chase: Summers at Shinnecock 1891–1902* (Washington D.C.: National Gallery of Art, 1987), passim; Ronald Pisano, *Long Island Landscape Painting,* 112–114.

18. "We are up here in another old corner of Connecticut….There are some very large oaks and chestnuts and many fine hedges. Lyme, or Old Lyme as it is usually called, is at the mouth of the Connecticut River and it really is a pretty fine old town." Hassam to J. Alden Weir, July 17, 1903 quoted in Barbara Novak and Annette Blaugrund, eds., *Next to Nature: Landscape Paintings from the National Academy of Design* (New York: National Academy of Design, 1980), 172; for Hassam at Old Lyme, see Susan G. Larkin, "Hassam in New England: Old Lyme" in Weinberg et al, *Childe Hassam*, 155–163.

19. For the art colony at Old Lyme, see Jeffrey W. Andersen, "The Art Colony at Old Lyme," in Spenser, Larkin, and Andersen, *Connecticut and American Impressionism*, 114–137, 160–161; H. S. Adams, "Lyme—A Country Life Community," *Country Life in America* (April 1914): 47–50, 92–94.

20. Jack Becker, "William Chadwick," in Peters and Lukehart, 78; Richard H. Love, *William Chadwick, 1879–1962: An American Impressionist* (Chicago: R. H. Love Galleries, 1978): 57, 61, 82; Gerdts, *American Impressionism* (1984): 224–226; H. S. Adams, "Lyme—A Country Life Community," *Country Life in America* (April 1914), 94.

21. Susan G. Larkin, [forthcoming] *Matilda Browne: Idylls of Farm and Garden* (Old Lyme, CT: Florence Griswold Museum, 2017); "Matilda Browne," in Andersen, Gerdts, and Harrison 1989, 39–40; May B. Hill, *The American Impressionists in the Garden*, 19; Barbara Mac Adam, "Matilda Browne" in Jeffrey W. Andersen, *Old Lyme: The American Barbizon* (Old Lyme, CT: Lyme Historical Society, Florence Griswold Museum, 1982), 35; see also note 7. *Peonies* has been identified as the garden of a fellow Old Lyme artist, Katharine Ludington, who went on to later fame as a suffragette.

22. May Brawley Hill, *The American Impressionists in the Garden*, 11–12; Deirdre Cunningham, "Ernest Lawson," in Marjorie B. Searle, ed., *Seeing America: Painting and Sculpture from the Collection of the Memorial Art Gallery of the University of Rochester* (Rochester: University of Rochester Press, 2006): 176–179; Valerie Ann Leeds, *Ernest Lawson* (New York: Gerald Peters Gallery, 2000), 28–30; John Wallace Gillies, "A Terrace Garden for Mr. H. H. Rogers at Tuxedo Park, New York: Walker & Gillette, Architects," *Country Life in America* 29 (November 1913): 36–37.

23. Joshua Ruff, *Gilding the Coast: Art & Design of Long Island's Great Estates* (Stony Brook, NY: The Long Island Museum of American Art, History and Carriages, 2015), 19–25; May Brawley Hill, *The Impressionists in the Garden*, 7; Ronald G. Pisano, *William de Leftwich Dodge: Impressions Home and Abroad* (New York: Beacon Hill Fine Art, 1998), 13–18; Lisa N. Peters, "William de Leftwich Dodge," in Peters and Lukehart, 136, 137; Gerdts, *Monet's Giverny*, 146, 147; 216, 238n., 245; Marjorie Balge, "William de Leftwich Dodge: American Renaissance Artist," *Art & Antiques* (January–February, 1982), 103; Gustav Kobbe, "Ancient Greece Reproduced in Long Island Villa," *New York Herald Magazine Section*, Sunday (August 14, 1910), 11.

24. The large cast of MacMonnies's *Pan of Rohallion*, originally commissioned for Adams and now in a private collection, is on loan to The Metropolitan Museum of Art (Thayer Tolles, ed., *American Sculpture in the Metropolitan Museum of Art*, vol. 1 (New York: Metropolitan Museum of Art, 1999), 428–429; Janis Conner and Joel Rosenkranz, *Rediscoveries in American Sculpture: Studio Works, 1893–1939* (Austin: University of Texas Press, 1989), 126, 132; For Dodge's reduced cast inscribed by MacMonnies, see: Ruff, *Gilding the Coasts*, 22; Pisano, *William De Leftwich Dodge*, 14; Susan E. Menconi, *Carved and Modeled: American Sculpture: 1810–1940* (New York: Hirschl & Adler Galleries, 1982), 64–65. For the marble torso, known as the "Dodge Venus," see Ruff, *Gilding the Coasts*, 22–24.

25. Thayer Tolles, ed., *American Sculpture in the Metropolitan Museum of Art*, vol. 2 (New York: Metropolitan Museum of Art, 2001), 566–567.

26. Anne Higonnet, "Anna Hyatt Huntington, Meet New York City," in *Goddess, Heroine, Beast: Anna Hyatt Huntington's New York Sculpture, 1902–1936* (New York: The Miriam & Ira D. Wallach Art Gallery, Columbia University in the City of New York, 2014), 17–20; Conner and Rosenkranz, *Rediscoveries in American Sculpture*, 74. For American garden sculpture, see Michele E. Bogart and Deborah Nevins, *Fauns and Fountains: American Garden Statuary: 1890–1930* (Southampton: The Parrish Art Museum, 1985).

27. For American parks as a modern life painting subject, see: James Glisson, "American Impressionism and the Problem of Urban Parks" in Marley, *The Artist's Garden*, 97–100, 102–103; Carol Osborne, "City Parks and Private Gardens in *Paintings of Modern America, 1875–1920*," in Betsy G. Fryberger et al, *The Changing Garden: Four Centuries of European and American Gardens* (Berkeley: Cantor Arts Center in association with the University of California Press, 2003), 62–73; Gallati, *William Merritt Chase: Modern American Landscapes*, 61–78, 111–136; "Painters of Modern Life in the Age of Great Cities" in Weinberg, Bolger and Curry, *American Impressionism and Realism*, 134–155.

28. H. Barbara Weinberg, "Hassam in New York, 1889–1896" in Weinberg et al, *Childe Hassam*, 110–112; Warren Adelson, "Cosmopolitan and Patriot" in Adelson, Cantor, and Gerdts, *Childe Hassam*, 41–43, 45.

29. H. Barbara Weinberg, "Hassam's Travels, 1892–1914," in Weinberg et al, *Childe Hassam*, 178–181; William H. Gerdts, "Three Themes: The City," in Adelson, Cantor, and Gerdts, *Childe Hassam*, 152–153; Terra Foundation for American Art: Collections discusses the circumstances of the commission as does May Brawley Hill, *The American Impressionists in the Garden*, 18. For the Wooded Island, see Wim de Wit, "Building an Illusion: The Design of the World's Columbian Exposition" in Neil Harris, Wim de Wit et al, *Grand Illusions: Chicago's World's Fair of 1893* (Chicago: Chicago Historical Society, 1993), 93; For Olmsted's critical role in selecting and planning the site for the World's Columbian Exposition, as well as his vision of the Lagoon and the Wooded Island as naturalistic counterpoints to the formality of the rest of the exposition grounds, see David Schuyler, "Frederick Law Olmsted and the World's Columbian Exposition," *Journal of Planning History*, vol. 15, no. 1 (February, 2015), 3–28.

FIGURE 21

Childe Hassam
Roses in a Vase, 1890
Oil on canvas, 20 x 24 in.
The Baltimore Museum of Art
Helen and Abram Eisenberg
Collection (BMA 1967.36.3)

Sense of Place, Sense of Spirit: Childe Hassam and Celia Thaxter on the Isles of Shoals

David Park Curry, Ph.D.

At first glance, Childe Hassam's luscious impression of somewhat blown tea roses in a glass vase seems an unlikely battle standard [fig. 21]. Just back from Europe, Hassam was gaining traction as an up-and-coming American Impressionist who would spend his long career battling for aesthetic beauty in an era marked by social, economic, and cultural upheaval. As artists struggled to address new audiences using ever-changing artistic standards, his fragile bouquet, set against a richly painted yet almost abstract background, hoists the banner of art for art's sake. Here, Hassam signaled his commitment to light, color, texture, indeed all that makes painting beautiful.

Hassam painted the roses in Celia Laighton Thaxter's cottage on Appledore Island, one of the Isles of Shoals off the coast of New Hampshire [fig. 22]. A lighthouse keeper's daughter who became a noted journalist and poet, Thaxter served as an aesthetic beacon, attracting 19th-century artists, writers, and musicians—including Ralph Waldo Emerson, Nathaniel Hawthorne, Henry Wadsworth Longfellow, Sarah Orne Jewett, and John Greenleaf Whittier, as well as composer John Knowles Paine and painter William Morris Hunt—to her family's resort hotel at the Shoals. Select guests climbed the cottage stairs to join Thaxter on the porch or in the parlor where she celebrated progressive art, music, and literature in a beautiful natural environment [fig. 23]. Once deemed the most idiosyncratic watering place in the Union, Appledore became the prototype for early 20th-century American summer art colonies.[1] Inspired by the parlor's cultured atmosphere, the garden's brilliant color, and the landscape's wild beauty, Hassam created some of his finest work there, tailoring the lessons of French Impressionism to his own purposes [fig. 24].[2]

Hassam's freely brushed still life echoes monochromatic bouquets that Thaxter gathered from her cottage garden on Appledore. Commissioned to illustrate her book, *An Island Garden* (1894), Hassam produced exquisite watercolors and oil paintings, many painted *en plein air*. In a painting likely inspired by a photograph, he captured Thaxter amidst her beloved blossoms near the garden's west gate for the book's frontispiece [figs. 25, 26].[3] She appears as a solid yet graceful figure lost in reverie in this painting.

FIGURE 22

Celia Thaxter's garden, Appledore, 1905
Portsmouth Athenaeum

Impressionism: American Gardens on Canvas

FIGURE 23

Childe Hassam
*Celia Thaxter's Garden, Appledore,
Isles of Shoals*, ca.1890
Oil on canvas, 13 x 9½ in.
Property of the Westervelt Collection
and displayed in the Tuscaloosa
Museum of Art in Tuscaloosa, Alabama

Blue outlining defines the board fence, as well as head, hands, and figure—right down to the silver crescent-shaped comb Thaxter wore in her hair. In contrast, the flowers are a painterly accumulation of pigments dragged over and through one another to create a sense of luxuriant bloom. Sometimes Hassam loaded the brush with several colors at once, to entangle them in a single stroke.

Enlivened by Hassam's imagery, Thaxter's colloquial, sometimes humorous, often exalted text came in the wake of Charles Dudley Warner's *My Summer in a Garden* (1870), a book that introduced a first-person voice into the encyclopedic garden literature of the Victorian era. Garden writer Michael Pollan has since characterized Warner's work as "over the back fence conversation."[4] Watching over her own 15 x 50-foot plot gave Thaxter rich material for passages in *An Island Garden*. "Mrs. Thaxter's pen-pictures" are still so vivid that it is possible in reading them to envision quite clearly what poet and painter chatted about on his visits to the Isles of Shoals.

Early on, Thaxter noticed how tiny crescent-shaped seeds eventually yielded marigolds, each flower "a mimic sun."[5] She later applied this metaphor of crescent growing into full-rayed orb in a sonnet acknowledging Hassam's talents as a painter.[6] As practical as she was poetic, Thaxter occasionally provided the young artist with savvy counsel. After she advised him to drop his prosaic first name, "Frederick," he started using a crescent cypher inspired by her silver hair ornament in his far more exotic—and easily remembered—signature, "Childe Hassam."[7] With Thaxter as muse, Hassam developed sharp powers of observation on his summer visits to Appledore, rendering multiple oils, watercolors, and pastels charged with a sense of nature's power as glorified in Thaxter's lyrical prose. A critic commented that Hassam's paintings gave "the world which cannot get to Appledore Island an idea of the peculiar wealth of color which the marine atmosphere, or else some fairy spell of the place, lends to the poppies and marigolds which grow in the poet's garden."[8]

In Hassam's Shoals pictures, the painterly allure of French Impressionism is readily apparent, yet he was also heir to complex ideas regarding "truth to Nature" advanced by John Ruskin, the leading English art critic of the Victorian era. Ruskin's emphasis on connections among nature, art, and society—expressed in

FIGURE 24

Karl Thaxter (attributed)
Childe Hassam painting a watercolor on the porch of Celia Thaxter's home, ca. 1886
Portsmouth Athenaeum

Impressionism: American Gardens on Canvas

FIGURE 25

Celia Thaxter picking flowers,
ca. 1892
Portsmouth Athenaeum

FIGURE 26

Childe Hassam
In the Garden, 1892
Oil on canvas, 22 1/8 x 18 1/8 in.
Smithsonian American Art Museum
Gift of John Gellatly (1929.6.52)

Impressionism: American Gardens on Canvas

FIGURE 27

Childe Hassam
*Celia Thaxter's Garden, Isles of
Shoals, Maine*, 1890
Oil on canvas, 17 ¾ x 12 ½ in.
The Metropolitan Museum of Art
Anonymous Gift (1994.567)

influential works such as his five-volume *Modern Painters* (1843–1860)—were explored by American artists of the generation preceding Hassam. They sought to privilege the individual artist's response to the natural world.[9] Ruskin's ideas remained current among many of the Boston Brahmins who sojourned in the carefree, rustic atmosphere on Appledore. Of course, Ruskin's principles were discussed in Thaxter's parlor and she quoted him freely in *An Island Garden.* Like Ruskin, she carefully examined flowers to know them better, but avoided scientific analysis in favor of description that offered a pathway to imaginative sensibility.

Within the garden, raised beds accommodated a range of what Thaxter called "the flowers our grandmothers loved."[10] But she also planted hundreds of poppies outside the fence, tumbling down the rocky slope towards the sea.[11] Her multiple paragraphs on poppies in *An Island Garden* are paralleled by Hassam's myriad images.[12] A lavish oil anchors viewers familiar with the Shoals with a site-specific glimpse of Babb's Rock in the center [fig. 27]. But the entire foreground is a visual opiate of dazzling poppies. In each one Thaxter perceived "a diamond of flame in a cup of gold. It is not enough that the powdery anthers are orange bordered with gold; they are whirled about the very heart of the flower like a revolving Catherine-wheel of fire."[13] The fireworks, whether written or visual, are intoxicating.

In the decades preceding American Impressionism, enormous machine paintings of regal mountain vistas by Frederic Edwin Church, Thomas Moran, and others gave way to the commercial viability of the oil sketch and the dominance of closely observed local incident over large national themes.[14] Thaxter's plot and Hassam's paintings appeared during the tumultuous period when— as the United States emerged as a major global economic power— Americans' relationship to the landscape gradually changed. In the face of urban development and attendant pollution, old-fashioned cottage gardens were a Colonial Revival antidote to the fast pace of modern life. Victorian families used greenhouses and terrariums to bring nature indoors for study and enjoyment [fig. 28].[15] Small objects of decorative art regularly reinforced engagement with the natural world, as in the case of a vase shaped like an anthropomorphic turtle carrying a festively-colored jack-in-the-pulpit, which conjures a city-dwelling child on an outing to gather natural specimens for a Victorian parlor [fig. 29], a practice Thaxter herself engaged in.[16]

Away from home, Americans experienced nature through the founding of the national park system, the growth of natural history museums and botanical gardens—including The New York Botanical Garden (1891)—as well as expanding tourism, and an explosion of articles in the popular press.[17] The challenges of describing and celebrating the natural world were eagerly embraced by writers and painters alike. Even environmentalist John Muir, whose elegant prose helped engender public support for establishing national parks,

FIGURE 28

Wardian Case (Terrarium), 1860–1880
Probably English
Painted and gilded cast iron, glass,
55 ½ x 26 ½ x 17 in.
The Baltimore Museum of Art
Charlotte B. Filbert Bequest Fund
(BMA 2007.186)

FIGURE 29

Karl L.H. Muller for the Union Porcelain Works, Greenpoint (Brooklyn), New York. *Turtle with Jack-In-The-Pulpit Vase*, ca. 1879
Porcelain with under and overglaze decoration, 8 ¼ x 4 ⅛ x 3 ½ in.
The Baltimore Museum of Art
Purchase with exchange funds from the Mary Frick Jacobs Collection
(BMA 1997.127.1)

> Both Thaxter and Hassam practiced careful scrutiny of nature, but it served as a springboard for the imagination.

understood the difficulty of pinning down the beauties of the natural world. In *The Mountains of California,* published the same year as *An Island Garden*, Muir noted:

> Fresh beauty opens one's eyes wherever it is really seen, but the very abundance and completeness of the common beauty that besets our steps prevents its being absorbed and appreciated.[18]

In a similar vein, Thaxter focused on a poppy seed that:

> …lies in your palm, [a] hardly visible…pin's point in bulk, but within it is imprisoned a spirit of beauty ineffable, which will break its bonds and emerge from the dark ground and blossom in a splendor so dazzling as to baffle all powers of description.[19]

Both Thaxter and Hassam practiced careful scrutiny of nature, but it served as a springboard for the imagination, triggering not only poetic language but also painted images that sidestep natural grandeur's potential for sensory overload. Like the work of many of his American Impressionist peers, Hassam's suggestive abstraction favors intimate personal experience, furthered by the relatively small scale of his works from the Isles of Shoals.

As Thaxter wrote, "the eternal sound of the sea on every side has a tendency to wear away the edge of human thought and perception; sharp outlines become blurred and softened like a sketch in charcoal."[20] In a breezily rendered pastel, Hassam conveyed an invigorating offshore wind tossing delicate flower heads [fig. 30]. Layers of pigment form a sensuous surface that takes on an abstract life of its own with colors still bold and fresh, offering us not so much a record of place as an intimation of spirit, communicating what it was to pause for a moment amidst such resplendent blossoms.

After Thaxter's death late in the summer of 1894, Hassam stayed away from the Shoals for several years. On his return, his work was dominated by seascapes recording the compelling confrontation of ancient rocks against relentless waters. By contrasting nature's temporal and enduring aspects, Hassam invested his work with lasting strength. A tiny pond centers *Summer Sea, Isles of Shoals* [fig. 31]. Hassam spun the composition around one of the brilliant turquoise tidal pools that were temporarily trapped in granite hollows, "like bits of fallen rainbow."[21] Offering a touch of transient beauty, this elusive jewel among the rocks will be gone almost as quickly as one of Thaxter's poppies faded in her garden. Like fingers, rocky ledges stretch tenuously into the vast ocean, much as poet and artist reached out for both an understanding of, and a relationship to, the natural world around them.

FIGURE 30

Childe Hassam
Isles of Shoals, ca. 1890
Pastel, 9 3/4 x 12 1/4 in.
Private Collection, Ohio
Courtesy of Keny Galleries

FIGURE 31

Childe Hassam
Summer Sea, Isles of Shoals, 1902
Oil on canvas, 25 3/16 x 30 5/16 in.
The Toledo Museum of Art, Toledo,
Ohio, Gift of Florence Scott Libbey,
1912.13

DAVID PARK CURRY, Ph.D., is Senior Curator of Decorative Arts and American Painting and Sculpture at the Baltimore Museum of Art.

1. For "idiosyncratic," see Samuel Adams Drake, *A Book of New England Legends and Folk Lore in Prose and Poetry.* (Boston: Little, Brown, and Company, 1901), p. 348. Trevor Fairbrother discussed the Shoals as a summer colony prototype in *The Bostonians: Painters of an Elegant Age, 1870–1930* (Boston: Museum of Fine Arts, 1986), p. 47.

2. David Park Curry, *Childe Hassam: An Island Garden Revisited.* (New York: W. W. Norton, 1990, reprinted 2004). Hassam had traveled to the Shoals by 1885. Created over nearly thirty years, his 400 Shoals images in various mediums comprise about 10% of his oeuvre.

3. Celia Laighton Thaxter, *An Island Garden* (Boston: Houghton, Mifflin and Company, 1894). The roses were picked in Thaxter's garden. Her "Plan of the Garden," opposite p. 72, includes a group of tea roses. Hassam's watercolor headpiece of yellow blossoms titled *Tea Roses* appears on p. 69. Thaxter discussed her flower arrangements at length, pp. 94–101. For Hassam's illustrations of her parlor and flower arrangements, see *The Altar and Shrine*, opposite p. 94, and *A Favorite Corner*, opposite p. 100.

4. http://michaelpollan.com/interviews/my-summer-in-a-garden, accessed 10/27/2015.

5. Thaxter, *Island Garden*, iii–vi. Thaxter is quoting Robert Browning, "Rudel to the Lady of Tripoli," 1842.

6. "A crescent with its glory just begun/ A spark from the great central fires sublime,/ A crescent that shall orb into a sun,/ And burn in splendor through the mists of time." Thaxter's handwritten copy, dated 1890, is bound into a copy of her book, *The Cruise of Mystery and Other Poems* now in the Rare Books Department of the Boston Public Library.

7. Hassam later recalled, "When I was not much past twenty I met Celia Thaxter who… said to me one day, 'you should not, with an unusual name like yours, fail to take advantage of its unique character—there is a young Englishman who has just written some remarkably good stories of India…his name is Joseph Rudyard Kipling—but he has dropped the prefix. If your name is to become known… it would be better without the F.'" Childe Hassam to Farmer, February 22, 1933, cited in Susan Faxon et. al., *A Stern and Lovely Scene: A Visual History of the Isles of Shoals* (Durham: N.H.: University Art Galleries, University of New Hampshire, 1978), p. 115.

8. Undated review of a Hassam exhibition of pastels and watercolors held in the late 1880s at Doll and Richards, Boston, cited in *Stern and Lovely Scene*, p. 118.

9. Studies include Linda S. Ferber, "Determined Realists: The American Pre-Raphaelites and the Association for the Advancement of Truth in Art" in Linda S. Ferber and William H. Gerdts, *The New Path: Ruskin and the American Pre-Raphaelites* (Brooklyn Museum, Brooklyn, New York, 1985), pp. 11–38. See also Susan P. Casteras, *English Pre-Raphaelitism and its Reception in America in the Nineteenth Century* (Rutherford: Fairleigh Dickinson University Press, 1990). For discussion of Hassam's relation to Ruskin, see Curry, *An Island Garden Revisited*, pp. 81–86, 91–92.

10. Thaxter, *An Island Garden*, p. 44. For a study, see May Brawley Hill, *Grandmother's Garden: The Old-Fashioned American Garden 1865–1915* (New York: Harry N. Abrams, 1995).

11. "I am always planting Shirley Poppies somewhere! One never can have enough of them, and by putting them into the ground at intervals of a week, later and later, one can secure a succession of blooms …to enjoy the livelong summer." Thaxter, *An Island Garden*, p. 50.

12. Thaxter thought that "for wondrous variety, for certain picturesque qualities, for color and form and subtle mystery of character, poppies seem the most satisfactory flower among the annuals. There is no limit to their variety of color," *An Island Garden*, p. 79. She waxed eloquent for the next seven pages. By the turn of the 20th century poppies, which dominate Hassam's floral imagery at the Shoals, would become a major icon of Art Nouveau style. Discussed, Curry, *An Island Garden Revisited*, pp. 81ff.

13. Thaxter, *An Island Garden*, p. 271.

14. While outdoor oil sketching was always an integral part of landscape painting, the display of oil sketches at the National Academy of Design, the American Art-Union, and elsewhere gradually resulted in sketches being collected for their own sake. Eleanor Harvey, *The Painted Sketch: American Impressions from Nature 1830–1880* (Dallas: The Dallas Museum of Art, 1998). See especially "The Oil Sketch on Display," and "Collecting the Painted Sketch," pp. 47–82.

15. Coal polluted the air in Victorian cities but Wardian cases protected delicate plants, spurring the craze for growing orchids and ferns indoors. In 1842, Nathaniel Bagshaw Ward published *On the Growth of Plants in Closely Glazed Cases.* His designs facilitated the transfer of exotic plants from the New World to the Old, eventually revolutionizing the international mobility of commercially important plants. Such devices became popular features in well-to-do households on both sides of the Atlantic.

16. Thaxter's album of pressed seaweeds and a necklace she made out of tiny shells survive at the Houghton Library, Harvard University. For illustrations, see Curry, *An Island Garden Revisited*, pp.36, 41, 43. Native to the moist woodlands and thickets of eastern North America, jack-in-the-pulpit is known by many picturesque common names such as bog onion, brown dragon, and American wake robin. For Thaxter on personable toads, her allies against garden pests, see *An Island Garden*, pp. 9–10.

17. Yellowstone Park was established in 1872. Sequoia and Yosemite followed in 1890. After the turn of the century, between 1900 and 1909, President Theodore Roosevelt authorized five more parks along with eighteen national monuments, four national game refuges, fifty-one bird sanctuaries, and over 100 million acres of national forest.

18. John Muir, *The Mountains of California* (1894) chapter 15. See file:///C:/Users/dcurry/Downloads/Muir_1894_-_The_Mountains_of_California%20(1).pdf. accessed 11/10/2015.

19. Thaxter, *An Island Garden*, p. 3.

20. Thaxter, *An Island Garden*, p. 13.

21. Thaxter, *Among the Isles of Shoals.* (Boston: James R. Osgood & Co., 1873), p. 124. For a discussion of the seascapes, dating from 1899 until about 1916, see Curry, "The Rocks of Appledore," *An Island Garden Revisited*, pp. 114–189.

Impressionism: American Gardens on Canvas

FIGURE 32

Edmund William Greacen
In Miss Florence's Garden, 1913
Oil on canvas, 30 x 30 in.
Private Collection

In Miss Florence's Garden: Edmund Greacen at Old Lyme

Susan G. Larkin, Ph.D.

"I have a pleasant family, Mr. & Mrs. Greacen, who will remain all winter. They are very nice indeed. Mr. Greacen knew all the men abroad & paints exceedingly well. Mrs. G. is very sweet & they have a dear little boy who is the delight of the house." So Florence Griswold, the doyenne of the art colony in Old Lyme, Connecticut, wrote to a friend on November 3, 1910.[1]

Edmund William Greacen had had ample opportunity to meet "all the men abroad." After completing his studies at William Merritt Chase's School of Art in New York, he married fellow student Ethol Booth of New Haven and with her joined Chase and other young artists on a trip to Spain. The Greacens continued their European travels after the tour, eventually settling in Paris, where their son was born in 1906.[2]

The following year, Greacen rented a house across from the train station in Giverny, the village where Claude Monet planted and painted his gardens. The Greacens became close friends of Monet's stepdaughter Marthe and her American husband, Theodore Butler, but met the French master only once. Since the late 1880s, Giverny had been inundated with artists, most of them American, eager to paint in Monet's shadow. Monet befriended only a few and even considered moving to escape them, but the art colony thrived nonetheless.[3]

Although Monet's garden was in effect off limits to them, the Americans in Giverny cultivated their own properties. The terraced garden surrounding the home of Mary Fairchild MacMonnies and sculptor Frederick MacMonnies was, one visitor declared, "the most beautiful . . . in the village," surpassing even Monet's.[4] Mary's painting depicts the upper terrace, recording its box-edged flower beds, gravel paths, and circular pool ornamented with an antique figure of Pan [fig. 33].[5] Their visitor William de Leftwich Dodge later adapted the effect for his own garden on Long Island, using a cast of the same sculpture to center a bed of irises [fig. 14].

> Greacen, MacMonnies, and others of the Giverny group used gardens as outdoor studios.

Impressionism: American Gardens on Canvas

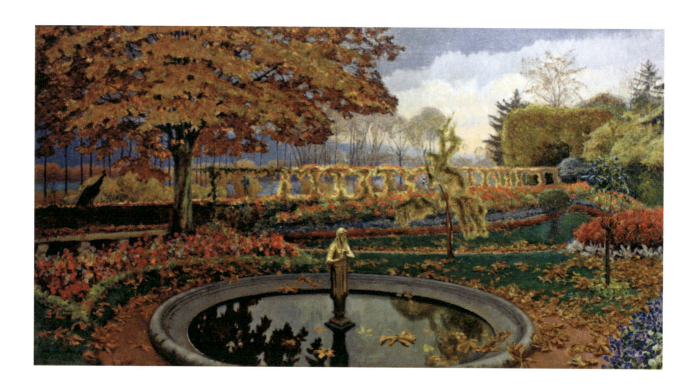

FIGURE 33

Mary Fairchild MacMonnies
Giverny Garden, ca. 1900
Oil on canvas
Sheldon Swope Art Gallery,
Terre Haute, Indiana

Greacen, MacMonnies, and others of the Giverny group used gardens as outdoor studios. Women in the garden, either fashionably dressed or nude, became a signature theme. Ethol Greacen frequently posed for her husband while arranging flowers, drifting in a rowboat, or enjoying a garden setting [fig. 34].

The Greacen family, by then also including a one-year-old daughter, returned to New York in 1909. The following year, they made their first visit to Old Lyme, where, as in Giverny, they enjoyed congenial company and stimulating subject matter. The artist colony in Old Lyme originated in emulation of another favored painting site in France: the village of Barbizon, the home of French masters Jean-François Millet and Théodore Rousseau.[6] American artist Henry Ward Ranger discerned a similarity between the rustic landscape of Barbizon near the Forest of Fontainebleau and the rocky hillsides of Old Lyme. In 1900 he enticed friends to join him, staying at the handsome but dilapidated mansion where Florence Griswold welcomed paying guests. Miss Florence, as she was known, was descended from a prominent family that included two governors of Connecticut [fig. 35]. She had received the education of a socially elite young woman yet struggled to make ends meet. To do so, she gave lessons in music, French, and needlework and advertised pansies and roses she propagated in her garden, as well as opening her historic home to boarders.[7] Her charm and empathy for her "boys," as she called the artists, made her the perfect hostess. Like Celia Thaxter in Appledore, she also served as an informal dealer, hanging her boarders' work in her spacious front hall.[8]

Beginning in 1902, the annual summer exhibitions in Old Lyme attracted the attention of critics and alerted artists to a new opportunity to market their work. Childe Hassam arrived in 1903. He stayed for only a short time before moving on to Appledore, but the brightly colored canvas he left behind for the exhibition commanded attention among the brownish tones of the Barbizon-inspired paintings. Before long, Impressionism replaced Tonalism as Old Lyme's dominant style, and "the American Barbizon" was renamed "the American Giverny."

Until he bought his own house in East Hampton in 1919, Hassam spent most summers going from place to place in New England in search of inspiring subject matter. In Old Lyme, as in Cos Cob, the other Connecticut village where Hassam did significant work, he favored landscapes featuring earlier uses of the land over gardens such as Celia Thaxter's on Appledore Island, which he

FIGURE 34

Edmund William Greacen
Tea Time, Giverny, 1907
Oil on canvas, 40½ x 38 in.
Select Fine Art Gallery

FIGURE 35

Florence Griswold among blossoming laurel
Florence Griswold Museum

FIGURE 36

Childe Hassam with *Apple Trees in Bloom, Old Lyme* on his easel, painting in the orchard behind Florence Griswold's house, 1904
Florence Griswold Museum, Lyme Historical Society Archives

famously depicted in numerous studies. Hassam was photographed with *Apple Trees in Bloom, Old Lyme* on his easel as he painted in the orchard behind Florence Griswold's house [fig. 36]. In the background of his composition is the shed that served as his studio, one of several farm buildings that had been repurposed for the artists' use. A contemporary writer described the setting: "The upper part of the barn has been fitted up as a studio and there are 'shacks' by the brook, by the river, and in the orchard.... All of the studios are unpretentiousness itself; they are comfortable and rural, and no more is desired of them."⁹

In rendering the ramshackle shed, Hassam evoked its agricultural past without betraying any evidence of its new role. His energetic brushwork suggests a light breeze ruffling the blossoms on two apple trees and stirring the grass on the riverbank. Perhaps recalling that bucolic scene, he wrote to Florence Griswold in late April 1905, "I wish I might have appeared with the first buds.... However, if I may have my studio in the garden (that I had before) and a room I will be happy."¹⁰

Thanks partly to Hassam, the Old Lyme art colony was well known by the time Greacen arrived in 1910; he was a regular visitor until 1918.¹¹ He found an American counterpart to his favorite Giverny theme in Florence Griswold's garden [fig. 37].

The most elaborate part of the old-fashioned garden was behind the house, visible from a side porch as seen in a painting by fellow painter William Chadwick [fig. 38]. Ethol Greacen probably posed for Chadwick, as she did for her husband's view of the same garden. *In Miss Florence's Garden* [fig. 32] depicts Ethol, dressed in pale pink and carrying a pink parasol, standing at the edge of a path bordered with peonies and white and yellow flowers (possibly sweet alyssum and basket-of-gold). The path leads the eye to the model, who seems to be another blossom in the luxuriant garden. The straight lines and neutral colors of the house and barn in the background contrast

FIGURE 37

Edmund William Greacen plein-air painting with Ethol Booth Greacen Edmund W. Greacen papers, 1905–1949, Archives of American Art, Smithsonian Institution (9214)

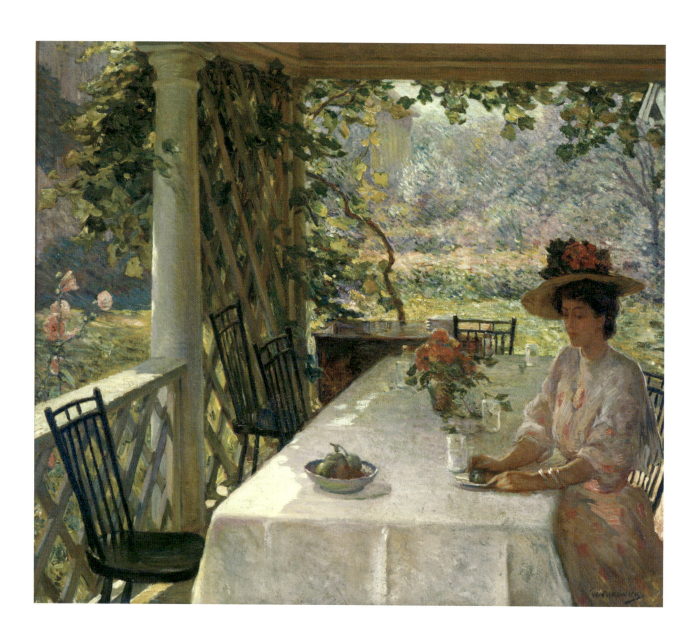

FIGURE 38

William Chadwick
On the Porch, ca. 1908–1910
Oil on canvas, 24 x 30 in.
Florence Griswold Museum
Gift of Mrs. Elizabeth Chadwick
O'Connell

FIGURE 39

Edmund William Greacen
The Old Garden, ca. 1912
Oil on canvas, 30 ¼ x 30 ¼ in.
Florence Griswold Museum
Gift of Mrs. Edmund Greacen, Jr.

FIGURE 40

William Chadwick
Irises, ca. 1908
Oil on canvas. 24 x 30 in.
Florence Griswold Museum
Gift of Elizabeth Chadwick O'Connell
(1975.7.5)

with the billowing plants. The soft-focus haziness, a characteristic of Greacen's work, prompted one of his students to ask, "Does Mr. Greacen look through a piece of gauze while he paints?"[12]

Greacen's choice of a square canvas for most of his garden paintings emphasizes the surface quality of his lively brushwork. In *The Old Garden* [fig. 39], another view of Miss Florence's perennial borders, his paint application varies from areas where the canvas is visible to thicker passages where the texture is built up. A pentimento just left of center reveals that the artist originally included a figure. By eliminating it, he reinforced the pattern of horizontal bands formed by flowers, lawn, and trees. He obscured the horizon line, immersing the viewer in the garden, where he played off the complementary colors of orange daylilies and blue delphinium. Instead of the overall view he chose for *In Miss Florence's Garden*, here he intimated the pleasure of discovering quiet corners. Greacen's paintings, along with contemporary photographs, guided the restoration of the garden that remains at the Florence Griswold Museum today.

Miss Florence's garden influenced others in Old Lyme as artists acquired their own properties nearby. According to a contemporary observer, "In the establishment of each of these offshoots of the Griswold house, 'Miss Florence' has taken a personal interest, extending even to the gardens, in which she has endeavored to infuse the air of yesteryear through the medium of the good old-fashioned flowers."[13]

The irises and lupines William Chadwick planted in his garden [fig. 40] surely met Miss Florence's approval as "good old-fashioned flowers." Clark Voorhees's garden provided subject matter both for him and Matilda Browne [fig. 41]. One can imagine the sharing of cuttings, seeds, and divisions among the artists and Miss Florence. The old-fashioned gardens in her orbit manifest a casual exuberance

FIGURE 41

Matilda Browne
In Voorhees's Garden, 1914
Oil on canvas, 20 x 26¼ in.
Florence Griswold Museum
Gift of the Hartford Steam Boiler
Inspection and Insurance Company
(2002.1.18)

in contrast to the rectilinear designs and bedding plants of the Victorian era as well as the Italianate style of the great estates then going up in wealthy enclaves around the country.

Partly through his exposure at Old Lyme's annual exhibitions, Greacen attracted commissions for "garden portraits." Some were intimate, such as the picture of the entrance to a house in Mamaroneck, New York, where the rhododendrons were in full bloom.[14] Others documented the gardens of great estates, including that of the Blue Garden of Arthur Curtiss James and Harriet James at Newport [fig. 42].[15] Designed by Frederick Law Olmsted, the Blue Garden was inaugurated in 1913 with a musical fete that was the first of many glittering social events held there over the next two decades. Planted entirely in a palette of blue, purple, white, and gray, it surrounded blue-tiled pools linked by a narrow channel evocative of Persian carpets. After decades of neglect, the garden has recently been restored and opened by appointment to visitors.[16] Greacen's portrait of the Blue Garden, which carefully records the overall design, is known today only through a black-and-white reproduction. Now that the garden itself has been restored, perhaps Greacen's early portrayal of it will come to light, revealing the full glory of his and Olmsted's vibrant palette.

FIGURE 42

Frances Benjamin Johnston
Blue Garden, Beacon Hill House,
Harriet and Arthur James,
Newport, Rhode Island, 1914
Library of Congress, Prints and
Photographs Division

SUSAN G. LARKIN, Ph.D., is an independent art historian and curator.

1. Florence Griswold (Old Lyme) to Schumacker Duncan (Washington, DC), November 3, Greacen file, 1910; Florence Griswold Museum.

2. The basic biography of Greacen is an essay by his granddaughter, Elizabeth Greacen Knudsen, in the exhibition catalogue *Edmund W. Greacen, N.A.: American Impressionist 1876–1949* (Jacksonville, Fla.: Cummer Gallery of Art, 1972).

3. See William H. Gerdts, *Monet's Giverny: An Impressionist Colony* (New York: Abbeville Press, 1993) and Bruce Weber, *The Giverny Luminists: Frieseke, Miller and Their Circle* (New York: Berry-Hill Galleries, Inc., 1995).

4. Quoted in May Brawley Hill, *On Foreign Soil: American Gardeners Abroad* (New York: Harry N. Abrams, 2005), p. 63. For another contemporary description of the MacMonnies garden, see William H. Gerdts, *Monet's Giverny: An Impressionist Colony*, 133.

5. I am grateful to Linda Ferber for bringing this information to my attention. For more information about the reproduction of the antique Pan figure that appears in paintings by Mary Fairchild MacMonnies Low and Dodge, see Hill, *Impressionists in the Garden*, 7; Gerdts, *Monet's Giverny*, 146, 147.

6. The most complete account of the Old Lyme art colony is Jeffrey W. Andersen's essay "The Art Colony at Old Lyme" in *Connecticut and American Impressionism* (Storrs: University of Connecticut, 1980), pp. 114–149. For more information, see *Old Lyme: The American Barbizon* (Florence Griswold Museum, 1982) and the website www.flogris.org.

7. Hildegard Cummings, "Florence Ann Griswold," Florence Griswold Museum website, accessed October 28, 2015: https://florencegriswoldmuseum.org/learn/our-history/miss-florence-scholar-essay/

8. For more on Celia Thaxter as an art dealer, see my essay "Hassam in New England" in H. Barbara Weinberg et al, *Childe Hassam: American Impressionist* (Metropolitan Museum of Art, 2004), pp. 124–126.

9. H. S. Adams, "Lyme—A Country Life Community," *Country Life in America* 25, no. 6 (April 1914), p. 46. For a reproduction of *Apple Trees in Bloom, Old Lyme* (1904, oil on panel, 25 x 30½ in., private collection), see H. Barbara Weinberg et al., *Childe Hassam: American Impressionist*, 158.

10. Childe Hassam (New York) to Florence Griswold (Old Lyme), April 29, 1905; archives, Florence Griswold Museum.

11. According to Knudsen (p. 10), Greacen visited Old Lyme every year between 1910 and 1913. It seems, however, that he spent more time there. He exhibited in Old Lyme every year from 1911 to 1917 and again in 1921. Although he was not necessarily in Old Lyme in each of those years, it is likely that he was. A letter addressed to him in Lyme in 1918 is evidence of his presence there that year.

12. Knudsen, p. 13.

13. Adams, p. 94.

14. William C. Dickerman (New York) to Edmund Greacen (Lyme) May 23, 1913; Archives of American Art, Greacen papers, roll 99.

15. Knudsen, p. 13. See also Mac Griswold and Eleanor Weller, *The Golden Age of American Gardens* (New York: Harry N. Abrams, 1991), pp. 101–102 (Pratt gardens), 134 (Taylor gardens), 9, 31, 33 (Blue Garden).

16. See http://thebluegarden.org and Arleyn Leves, "The Iconic Blue Garden of Newport," http://www.olmsted.org/news-and-publications/news/recent-naop-news/649-the-iconic-blue-garden-of-newport

FIGURE 43

John Singer Sargent
In the Luxembourg Gardens, 1879
Oil on canvas, 25 7/8 x 36 1/8 in.
Philadelphia Museum of Art
The John G. Johnson Collection, 1917

John Singer Sargent at Vizcaya and Pocantico Hills

Elaine Kilmurray

John Singer Sargent painted garden scenes early in his career, from studies of the Luxembourg Gardens in Paris [fig. 43] to flower and garden studies done in England in preparation for his painting of girls lighting Japanese lanterns at twilight, *Carnation, Lily, Lily, Rose* [fig. 44]. The majority of his garden scenes, however, were later, executed on annual painting campaigns in continental Europe in the early years of the 20th century. The subject of parks, gardens, garden architecture, and statuary is one of the most recurrent at this time in his career, when he was trying to reduce his portrait practice so that he could devote himself to his mural work for the Boston Public Library and paint what he chose, without the constraints of commissions. These garden pictures are an expression of his taste for the high style of the Renaissance, Mannerism, and the Baroque period. They reveal his passion for the artistic past— its informing spirit and cultural legacy—and they glance backwards to a personal past.

Sargent's peripatetic childhood was spent in pre-modern Europe. Italy, the country of his birth and the scene of much of his cultural education, formed his individual landscape of memory. Writer Vernon Lee (1856–1935), his childhood friend and partner in various cultural expeditions to Rome and Bologna, was herself a garden historian, and she wrote extensively about *genius loci,* particularly with regard to Italy. Lee attributed her own sensitivity to place to Sargent's redoubtable mother, whom she called the "most wisely fantastic of Wandering Ladies."[1]

Sargent's garden scenes are intimately related to his sense of place. Their appeal lay in aesthetic beauty, in the dialogue among art and nature, sculpture and vegetation, green spaces, stone and water, the contrasts of light and shade, but also in the sense of passing time embodied in them. Sargent found his subjects in royal palaces, private villas, and public parks in Spain, Portugal, and Italy. As a group these pictures reflect a contemporary sensibility with regard to gardens and garden architecture. They are a pictorial counterpart to works on garden design and history, such as the photographs in Charles Platt's

FIGURE 44

John Singer Sargent
Carnation, Lily, Lily, Rose, 1885–6
Oil on canvas, 68½ x 60½ in.
Tate, Presented by the Trustees of the Chantrey Bequest, 1887 (N01615)

Impressionism: American Gardens on Canvas

FIGURE 45

John Singer Sargent
Palmettos, 1917
Watercolor, graphite, and wax crayon
on white wove paper, 15 1/4 x 20 3/4 in.
The Metropolitan Museum of Art
Gift of Mrs. Francis Ormond
(501.130.65)

Italian Gardens (1894) and the chapters in Edith Wharton's *Italian Villas and Their Gardens* (1904).

The outbreak of war in the summer of 1914 effectively brought an end to Sargent's European excursions and the works of art they inspired. He spent much of the next decade in North America and set foot on the soil of continental Europe only once, when he went to the Western Front as a war artist in 1918. However, during this time, an echo of the European garden came to him in two of its most ambitious American reincarnations.

In February 1917, he was in Florida making a rare exception to his embargo on portraiture by painting a portrait of John D. Rockefeller (1839–1937) at Ormond Beach.[2] He spent three weeks there, struggling with the sweltering heat and painting typical Floridian subjects, including alligators and palmettos [fig. 45], before moving on to Miami to stay with his old friend, industrialist Charles Deering (1852–1927), whom he had known since his student days in Paris.[3] Charles and his half-brother, James, were fabulously wealthy; they were Europhile in their tastes and audacious in their architectural and horticultural aspirations.

Charles Deering created an estate with a museum to house his art collection in Sitges, south of Barcelona in Spain; he built Buena Vista, a Spanish-influenced house north of Miami, and subsequently acquired land at Cutler (later absorbed into Palmetto Bay), south of Miami.[4] James Deering (1859–1925) bought 130 acres of land on Brickell Point, south of the Miami River in 1912, and planned to build a villa there, which he would call Vizcaya in honor of the Spanish adventurers who had sailed to America from the Basque province and had charted the south Floridian shoreline. It was a site of great natural beauty, but it was complicated and difficult terrain, part coral reef, part mangrove swamp, and part tropical hammock, and its position overlooking Biscayne Bay made it fatally vulnerable to storms and hurricanes. James and his advisors in the design of the property, artist Paul Chalfin, architect Francis Burrall Hoffman Jr, and garden designer Diego Suarez, had set out to create a house and gardens that imitated and evoked a vanishing European past [fig. 46]. The house was modeled on the Villa Rezzonico (ca. 1670) in Bassano del Grappa, which was the work of Baldessare Longhena, the same

FIGURE 46

Leda-Mound East Terrace,
Vizcaya, 1934
Frank Bell Photograph Collection,
Vizcaya Museum and Gardens
Archives, Miami, Florida

FIGURE 47

John Singer Sargent
Terrace, Vizcaya, 1917
Watercolor and graphite on
white wove paper, 13 ¾ x 21 in.
The Metropolitan Museum of Art
Gift of Mrs. Francis Ormond,
1950 (50.130.81n)

architect who had designed Santa Maria della Salute, the church at the entrance to the Grand Canal in Venice. With this Baroque style as its touchstone, it is unsurprising that Sargent was seduced upon his arrival at Vizcaya. He had long been captivated by the Salute, painting it in oil and watercolor. It was a site of great painterly significance for him.

Sargent painted a watercolor portrait of his host during the time he spent at Vizcaya, but it was the villa and grounds that entranced him. Ever since his arrival in America the previous year, he had "been hungering for some architectural painting."[5] This craving emanates from his lyrical, light-filled watercolors of the villa, harbor, and gardens, which have a dreamlike quality. He rendered the patio in close-up and painted views of the East terrace leading on from it with its balustrade, trees, and vases [fig. 47], and a view of the northern facade of the villa, with its wide terrace, urns, and sculpture. Beyond the terraces, the sense of fantasy intensified, and Sargent might

FIGURE 48

John Singer Sargent
Shady Paths, Vizcaya, 1917
Watercolor on paper, 15 ⅝ x 21 in.
Worcester Art Museum
Sustaining Membership Fund
(1917.88)

> "There is so much to paint… at my host's brother's villa. It combines Venice and Frascati and Aranjuez…"

almost have felt that he had arrived in Venice, the city closest to his artistic heart.

The Deerings were aesthetes, but they were also enlightened conservationists. James Deering planned the villa on a north-south axis, specifically so that the hammock to the north could be protected. The sylvan environment in *Shady Paths, Vizcaya* [fig. 48] represents part of this hammock. The trunks of live oaks and gumbo limbo trees and the dappled foliage create a dark, saturated backdrop for the 17th- and 18th-century marble statues of mythological and allegorical figures that stood on plinths in a small circular glade.[6] The pale statuary, luminous against the dense dark green, is reminiscent of the romantic melancholy of some of Sargent's representations of the Villa Torlonia at Frascati and the Boboli Gardens in Florence, empty of human life and peopled by ghostly statues. The gardens at Vizcaya that Sargent saw in 1917 were unfinished. Work on the entrance forecourt, the terraces to east and north and the hammock had been completed, but the great south gardens devised as a succession of "rooms" in the Italian manner were very much a work in progress. The continuing nature of the project is obliquely referenced in several sensuous studies of African-American workers relaxing in the sun under low-lying mangrove in an area of beach to the south of the house, now in the collections of the Worcester Art Museum and The Metropolitan Museum of Art. A wistful tone pervaded Sargent's correspondence at this time: "[…It] is hard to leave this place. There is so much to paint…at my host's brother's villa. It combines Venice and Frascati and Aranjuez and all that one is likely never to see again. Hence this linger-longering."[7]

In June an exhibition of Sargent's watercolors from this period, *Scenes in Florida where the Artist has been Staying for the Past Month or So,* was held at the Copley Gallery in Boston. Shortly after, Sargent traveled from Florida to Pocantico Hills, to paint a second portrait of Rockefeller at Kykuit, his estate north of New York City. John D. Rockefeller, Jr. had commissioned architects William Adams Delano and Chester Holmes Aldrich to design a country home for his father on a site high above the eastern bank of the Hudson River. William Welles Bosworth was to design the gardens (the three major players had all trained at the Ecole des Beaux-Arts in Paris). At a relatively early stage, the house was remodeled to rectify certain faults and a new facade, designed by Bosworth, was created. It became clear that the facade of the revised version demanded a proportionately impressive forecourt. J. D. Rockefeller, Jr. wrote to his father on May 10, 1913:

> […] Mr. Bosworth tells me that in his early talks with you he emphasized the fact that the central feature of the forecourt must be some large and commanding piece of sculpture […] He is convinced that nothing more splendid or appropriate

FIGURE 49

John Singer Sargent
Boboli Gardens, ca. 1906
Watercolor on paper, 10 x 14 in.
Brooklyn Museum, New York
Purchased by Special Subscription
(09.818)

could be suggested than the reproduction of a noted fountain in Florence, which would stand high above the ground and make a magnificent effect from the entrance of the house as one looks towards the east.[8]

The "noted fountain" was Giambologna's *Oceanus and The Three Rivers* [fig. 50], which is situated in the center of the Island Pond at the end of the Cypress Avenue, the principal axis of the Boboli Gardens. Giambologna's Neptune is a figure of tranquil authority, controlling and subduing his domain. Holding a conch shell to his left thigh, and a *bastone del comando* in his right hand, he stands, one foot resting on a dolphin, above three crouching figures (personifying the three rivers of the ancient world, the Nile, the Ganges, and the Euphrates), who pour water into the great basin beneath them.[9] Sargent knew the Boboli Gardens well, but he chose to paint the smaller statues around the pond, rather than the massive fountain, its centerpiece [fig. 49] He painted fountains elsewhere in Italy and Spain, but rarely represented the entire structure, choosing instead to narrow the field of vision and isolate a section or detail.[10] This selective framing demands engagement from the spectator, who is required to imagine a whole from the partial view. In some cases Sargent's inventive cropping was so bold as almost to exclude completely the monumental allegorical figures that formed the apex of the sculpture. Sargent portrayed the Oceanus fountain at Kykuit in a similar manner [fig. 51]. The composition is symmetrical: the great *tazza* almost fills the width of the canvas, but the figure of Neptune is cropped at the waist, so that the lower body and the figures of the river gods crouching beneath him become the focal point. He represents the fountain looking north (the house, out of frame, would have been to his left) and from a very low viewpoint. One of two urns on top of the balustrade marking the entrance to the eastern stairway, which leads down from the forecourt to a terrace below, is visible, and one of the six elm trees that shaded the forecourt is in the background.[11] A watercolor of a vase fountain on the south terrace at Kykuit [fig. 52] is, by comparison, a placid composition, ordered and anchored, fine jets of water spouting from the rim of a marble vase into a shallow basin against a background of variegated foliage.

Sargent responded to the gardens at Vizcaya and Kykuit poetically, inflecting the sites with his experiences and memories of the formal European gardens he had painted repeatedly and with a distinctive eye. They crystallize an elegance, grace, and high stylishness that he admired, and they breathe nostalgia for a European culture under threat and wonder at the confidence of an American elite creating for the future.

FIGURE 50

Giambologna, *Oceanus and the Three Rivers*, completed 1576, Boboli Gardens, Florence

FIGURE 51

John Singer Sargent
The Fountain of Oceanus, 1917
Oil on canvas, 27 ½ x 22 in.
Kykuit, The National Trust for
Historic Preservation, Bequest of
Laurance S. Rockefeller

ELAINE KILMURRAY
is an art historian and Research Director of the John Singer Sargent Catalogue Raisonné project.

1. Vernon Lee, *The Sentimental Traveller: Notes on Places* (London: John Lane, Bodley Head, 1908, 10–11). See *Genius Loci: Notes on Places* (London: Grant Richards, 1897) and *The Golden Keys and Other Essays on the Genius Loci* (London: John Lane, Bodley Head, 1925). For Vernon Lee's garden, 'Il Palmerino', near Florence, see Katie Campbell, *Paradise of Exiles: The Anglo-American Gardens of Florence* (London: Frances Lincoln Limited, 2009), 96–103.

2. The portrait of Rockefeller that Sargent painted at Ormond Beach is in a private collection. The second, painted at Pocantico Hills, is at Kykuit.

3. Sargent to Ariana Curtis, February 26 [1917], Sargent Papers, Library of the Boston Athenaeum.

4. For Deering's art center in Sitges, see Isabel Coll Mirabent's bilingual *Charles Deering and Ramón Casas: A Friendship in Art* (Evanston, Ill. Northwestern University Press, 2010).

5. James Deering to Paul Chalfin, 23 March 1917, Vizcaya Museum and Gardens Archive, Miami, Florida.

6. They have since been removed and repositioned in the grounds, owing to storm damage.

7. Sargent to his cousin, Mary Patterson Hale, 'The Sargent I Knew', *World Today*, 50 (November 1927): 569.

8. J.D. Rockefeller, Jr., to J. D. Rockefeller Sr., May 10, 1913, Rockefeller Archive Center, New York.

9. The fountain was a product of European and American craftsmanship. The figures, carved in Carrara marble, were made in Florence, and the granite bowl was quarried and carved on Crotch Island, Maine. The fountain was installed at Kykuit in July 1914, where it still dominates the entrance court.

10. Among the studies Sargent painted of fountains are: an oil of the Fountain of Neptune in the Piazza Vecchia, Florence (ca. 1902, The Art Institute of Chicago, Anonymous Loan, 313.1996); the Fountain of Triptolemus in the Jardin de la Isla, Aranjuez, in watercolor and oil (ca. 1903, Brooklyn Museum, New York, 09.809, and 1912, private collection); studies in oil and watercolor of the fountain at the Villa Torlonia. Frascati (1907, Art Institute of Chicago, 1914.57 and private collections); studies, in oil and watercolor of the Neptune Fountain in the main square in Bologna (ca. 1906, private collections); a watercolor of the Fontana dei Quattro Fiumi in Rome (1906, private collection), and watercolors of the Fountain in the main courtyard of the hospital of San Juan de Dios in Granada (1912, The Metropolitan Museum of Art, New York, 15.142.6, and Fitzwilliam Museum, Cambridge, PD. I–1971).

11. Sargent gave the painting to the St. Botolph Club in Boston in 1922. Twenty years later, Bosworth acted as intermediary between Rockefeller and the club to bring about Rockefeller's purchase of the picture.

FIGURE 52

John Singer Sargent
Vase Fountain, Pocantico, 1917
Watercolor, 21 x 15 in.
Private Collection

Checklist

HUGH HENRY BRECKENRIDGE
(1870–1937)
White Phlox, 1906
Oil on canvas, 30 x 25 in.
Terra Foundation for American Art
Daniel J. Terra Collection (1988.15)

MATILDA BROWNE (1869–1947)
Peonies, 1907
Oil on panel, 11½ x 14 in.
Florence Griswold Museum Purchase
(2013.11)

WILLIAM MERRITT CHASE
(1849–1916)
Park in Brooklyn, ca. 1887
Oil on panel, 16⅛ x 24⅛ in.
Parrish Art Museum, Water Mill, New York
Littlejohn Collection (1961.5.11)

DANIEL PUTNAM BRINLEY
(1879–1963)
The Peony Garden, 1912
Oil on canvas, 43¾ x 38¾ in.
Virginia Museum of Fine Arts, Richmond
Adolph D. and Wilkins C. Williams Fund

WILLIAM CHADWICK (1879–1962)
Irises, ca. 1908
Oil on canvas, 24 x 30 in.
Florence Griswold Museum
Gift of Elizabeth Chadwick O'Connell
(1975.7.5)

HENRI CRENIER (1873–1948)
Boy and Turtle, 1912
Bronze, 19¾ x 11 x 11 in.
The Metropolitan Museum of Art
Amelia B. Lazarus Fund, 1913 (13.87)

MATILDA BROWNE (1869–1947)
In Voorhees's Garden, 1914
Oil on canvas, 18 x 24 in.
Florence Griswold Museum
Gift of The Hartford Steam Boiler Inspection
and Insurance Company (2002.1.18)

WILLIAM MERRITT CHASE
(1849–1916)
Landscape: Shinnecock, Long Island,
ca. 1896
Oil on wood panel, 14⁵⁄₁₆ x 16⅛ in.
Princeton University Art Museum
Gift of Francis A. Comstock,
Class of 1919 (y1939-35)

MARIA OAKEY DEWING
(1845–1927)
Rose Garden, 1901
Oil on canvas, 24 x 40½ in.
Crystal Bridges Museum of American Art,
Bentonville, Arkansas (2006.67)

WILLIAM DE LEFTWICH DODGE (1867–1935)
The Artist's Garden, ca. 1916
Oil on canvas, 35 x 27 in.
Neville-Strass Collection

CHILDE HASSAM (1859–1935)
Descending the Steps, Central Park, 1895
Oil on canvas, 22⅜ x 22¼ in.
Virginia Museum of Fine Arts, Richmond
Gift of the Estate of Hildegarde Graham van Roijen (93.112)

ANNA VAUGHN HYATT HUNTINGTON (1876–1973)
Diana of the Chase, 1922
Bronze and marble, 99 x 33 x 29½ in.
The New-York Historical Society
Gift of Mr. and Mrs. Archer B. Huntington (1939.252)

EDMUND WILLIAM GREACEN (1877–1949)
In Miss Florence's Garden, 1913
Oil on canvas, 30 x 30 in.
Private Collection

CHILDE HASSAM (1859–1935)
Horticulture Building, World's Columbian Exposition, Chicago, 1893
Oil on canvas, 18½ x 26¼ in.
Terra Foundation for American Art
Daniel J. Terra Collection (1999.67)

ERNEST LAWSON (1873–1939)
The Garden, 1914
Oil on canvas, 20 x 24 in.
Memorial Art Gallery of the University of Rochester
Gift of the Estate of Emily and James Sibley Watson (51.36)

CHILDE HASSAM (1859–1935)
Celia Thaxter's Garden, Appledore, Isles of Shoals, ca. 1890
Oil on canvas, 13 x 9½ in.
Property of the Westervelt Collection and displayed in the Tuscaloosa Museum of Art in Tuscaloosa, Alabama

CHILDE HASSAM (1859–1935)
Old House and Garden, East Hampton, Long Island, 1898
Oil on canvas, 24¹⁄₁₆ x 20 in.
Henry Art Gallery, University of Washington, Seattle
Horace C. Henry Collection (26.70)

FREDERICK W. MACMONNIES (1863–1937)
Pan of Rohallion, 1890
Bronze, 29¾ x 9 x 10½ in.
Memorial Art Gallery of the University of Rochester
Anonymous gift (98.68)

JOHN SINGER SARGENT
(1856–1925)
The Fountain of Oceanus, 1917
Oil on canvas, 27½ x 22 in.
Kykuit, The National Trust for
Historic Preservation, Bequest of
Laurance S. Rockefeller

JOHN H. TWACHTMAN
(1853–1902)
Wildflowers, ca. 1890
Oil on canvas, 30¼ x 25¼ in.
Taubman Museum of Art
Acquired with funds provided by the
Horace G. Fralin Charitable Trust and
Partial Support from Spanierman Gallery,
LLC (1999.004)

JOHN SINGER SARGENT
(1856–1925)
Terrace, Vizcaya, 1917
Watercolor and graphite on white
wove paper, 13¾ x 21 in.
The Metropolitan Museum of Art
Gift of Mrs. Francis Ormond, 1950
(50.130.81n)

THEODORE WORES (1859–1939)
*Thomas Moran's House
(East Hampton, Long Island)*, ca. 1894
Oil on canvas board, 9 x 12 in.
The Heckscher Museum of Art
Gift of Dr. A. Jess Shenson
in memory of Ronald G. Pisano

JOHN SINGER SARGENT
(1856–1925)
Vase Fountain, Pocantico, 1917
Watercolor, 21 x 15 in.
Private Collection

Further Reading

Bailly, Austen Barron, et al. *American Impressionist: Childe Hassam and the Isles of Shoals*. New Haven: Yale University Press, 2016.

Curry, David Park. *Childe Hassam: An Island Garden Revisited*. New York: W.W. Norton, 2004.

Gerdts, William H. *American Impressionism*. New York: Abbeville Press, 1984.

___. *Monet's Giverny: An Impressionist Colony*. New York: Abbeville Press, 1993.

Hill, May Brawley. *The American Impressionists in the Garden*. Nashville, TN: Vanderbilt University Press, 2010.

___. *Grandmother's Garden: The Old-Fashioned American Garden, 1865–1915*. New York: Harry N. Abrams, Inc., 1995.

Kilmurray, Elaine and Warren Adelson. *Sargent and Impressionism*. New York: Adelson Galleries, 2010.

Larkin, Susan G. *The Cos Cob Colony: Impressionists on the Connecticut Shore*. New Haven: Yale University Press, 2001.

Marley, Anna O., ed. *The Artist's Garden: American Impressionism and the Garden Movement*. Philadelphia: University of Pennsylvania Press in association with the Pennsylvania Academy of Fine Arts, 2015.

Peters, Lisa N., et al. *Visions of Home: American Impressionist Images of Suburban Leisure and Country Comfort*. Carlisle, PA: The Trout Gallery, Dickinson College/University Press of New England, 1997.

Thaxter, Celia Laighton. *An Island Garden*. Boston: Houghton Mifflin and Company, 1894.

Weinberg, H. Barbara, Doreen Bolger, and David Park Curry. *American Impressionism and Realism: The Painting of Modern Life, 1885–1915*. New York: The Metropolitan Museum of Art, 1994.